8-15-80

Whether most people are aware of it or not, secular humanism — the philosophy that declares, "no deity will save us; we must save ourselves" — has been quietly woven into the fabric of our daily lives. Yet the danger signs are quite evident:

- legislation on the national level reflects widespread acceptance of easy divorce, abortion-on-demand, gay rights, militant feminism, unisex facilities, and leniency towards pornography, prostitution, and crime.

- the public school system has demonstrated hostility toward prayer, moral and religious values, creation as an alternative to evolution, and the teaching of sex education within a moral context.

- a sexually permissive, self-indulgent approach to life has become the norm for movies, books, and even prime time television.

In short, many religious leaders believe that America may very well follow in the footsteps of Sodom and Gomorrah.

What can concerned Christians do to fight back? Plenty, says Tim LaHaye, best-selling author and president of Family Life Seminars.

THE BATTLE FOR THE MIND is his shocking, detailed exposé of the humanist onslaught, as well as a positive, practical handbook for waging war against this subtle infiltration. The author maps out specific avenues you can take to restore God's standards to the institutions and influences that inevitably shape our thinking — and that of our children.

The war has already begun. As a Christian, you need to know how to win THE BATTLE FOR THE MIND.

The Battle for the Mind

Tim LaHaye

FLEMING H. REVELL COMPANY
OLD TAPPAN, NEW JERSEY

Unless otherwise indicated, Scripture quotations in this volume are from the King James Version of the Bible.

Scripture quotations identified NKJB—NT are from The New King James Bible—New Testament. Copyright © 1979, Thomas Nelson, Inc., Publishers.

Quotations from *Philosophy of Humanism,* by Corliss Lamont, copyright © 1949, 1957, 1965 by Corliss Lamont. Reprinted by permission of Frederick Ungar Publishing Company.

Material from *Humanist Manifestos I and II* was published by Prometheus Books, 1203 Kensington Ave., Buffalo, N.Y., and is reprinted by permission.

Excerpts from *The SIECUS Circle,* by Claire Chambers, Copyright © 1977 by Western Island. Used by permission.

Excerpts from *How Should We Then Live?* by Francis A. Schaeffer, © 1976 by Francis A. Schaeffer. Used by permission.

Library of Congress Cataloging in Publication Data

LaHaye, Tim F
   The battle for the mind.

   Includes bibliographical references.
   1. Apologetics—20th century. 2. Humanism—Controversial literature. 3. Atheism—Controversial literature. 4. United States—Moral conditions. 5. Christianity—Philosophy. I. Title.
BT1102.L255   211'.6   80-16832
ISBN 0-8007-1112-2
ISBN 0-8007-5043-8 (pbk.)

This book is dedicated to Dr. Francis Schaeffer, the renowned philosopher-prophet of the twentieth century. Although we have never met personally, I have admired him from a distance and greatly respect the enormous contribution his books, movies, seminars, and other teachings have made in the current awakening of our people to the dangers of humanism. I hope his warnings and those in this book are not too late.

2113499

Contents

Introduction

Scientists call the human mind "The most complex living mechanism in the world." It certainly is the most important, for as it goes, so goes the human being. God has given us four primary orbs with entrance to the mind, in order to influence it—two eyes and two ears. What you see and hear influence the thoughts of your mind; and your mind determines your actions.

In this world, there are two basic lines of reasoning that determine the morals, values, life-style and activities of mankind—the wisdom of man or the wisdom of God (*see* 1 Corinthians 1:17–25). Today they take the form of atheistic humanism or Christianity. What this life is all about is *THE BATTLE FOR YOUR MIND:* whether you will live your life guided by man's wisdom (humanism) or God's wisdom (Christianity). Either one will affect the way you live and where you spend eternity.

Most people today do not realize what humanism really is and how it is destroying our culture, families, country—and one day, the entire world. Most of the evils in the world today can be traced to humanism, which has taken over our government, the UN, education, TV, and most of the other influential things of life.

The church of Jesus Christ is the last obstacle for the humanists to conquer. The 1960s saw the battle for racial rights.

In the 1970s, it was sexual rights. But the 1980s have been designated for the battle against religious rights.

Unfortunately, at this time of destiny, the church is sound asleep, and unless the 60 million people who George Gallup's poll indicates are Christians wake up to who the enemy really is, the humanists will accomplish their goal of a complete world takeover by the year 2,000.

I believe there is yet time for us to defeat the humanists and reverse the moral decline in our country that has us on a collision course with Sodom and Gomorrah. I believe God will yet bless this nation and give us another great revival, which I call Great Awakening II. It will only come, however, if we become informed of what humanism is, who the enemy is, and how to fight their subtle form of religious evil.

This book is dedicated to explaining humanism in simple terms, so that the man on the street can both understand its danger and be motivated to oppose it at the place it can be defeated—the ballot box. We must remove all humanists from public office and replace them with pro-moral political leaders. The Bible says, "When the righteous are in authority, the people rejoice . . ." (Proverbs 29:2).

This is not a book of gloom, doom, and despair, but a clarion call to "saltless" Christians to fulfill Dr. Francis Schaeffer's challenge to:

- Continue being lights in the world, but also . . .
- Be a savoring moral influence in our culture.

You will find positive suggestions on what you can do to triumph over this religious evil and help return our country to moral sanity.

Note to teachers: For information regarding visual transparencies for use as teaching aids with overhead projection, write to Family Life Seminars, P.O. Box 1299, El Cajon, CA 92022.

THE BATTLE FOR THE MIND

1

Your Incredible Brain

Your brain is the most complex mechanism in the world and the most influential organ of your body. It accounts for your ability to think, remember, love, hate, feel, reason, imagine, and analyze. The principal difference between you and animals, it is one organ without which you cannot sustain life.

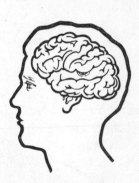 The average brain, weighing about 3 pounds, contains 12 billion cells, each of which is connected to 10,000 other brain cells, totaling 120 trillion brain connections. No wonder a scientist stated, "The human brain is the most complex arrangement of matter in the universe."[1] Some have compared the human brain to a sophisticated computer, but technology hasn't even come close to duplicating its capabilities. Dr. Gehard Dirks, who holds fifty patents on the IBM computer, told me that he acquired most of his inventive ideas from studying the functions of the human brain. Commenting on its complexity, he stated, "If we could invent a computer that would duplicate the capabilities of the human brain, it would take a structure the size of the Empire State Building, just to house it."

Your brain supervises everything you do, from the involuntary beat of your heart to the conscious decisions of life. It controls hearing, sight, smell, speech, eating, resting, learning, prejudices, and everything else that makes you behave as you do. The characteristics that you inherited at birth, which produce your unique traits, temperament, and even physical growth, are controlled by your brain.

We have little or no conscious control over many of these traits, and even today, scientists disagree as to the extent to which we exercise mastery over ourselves. One man I know, who went to his doctor because his heart was racing, discovered that fears in his mind caused his body to simulate a heart attack. By learning to govern his fears, he was able to control his heart.

In the case of malfunctioning sight, hearing, or other bodily impairments, it is not so simple, and yet our thoughts and feelings do indeed influence our behavior. The wise writer of Proverbs observed, "As a man thinks in his heart, so is he" (*see* Proverbs 23:7).

Most scientists agree that although we cannot consciously control all the functions of our brain, most people could regulate far more of them than they realize. One thing is certain: What you see, what you hear, and the way you think (your philosophy of life) are the most significant influences on your life. The following diagrams illustrate the three most important functions of your brain—your intellect, emotions, and will. These three areas are so interrelated that many people think of them as one. They are, in fact, independent; and as we shall see, your emotions and will are highly influenced by your intellect.

Your Mind

A major portion of your 1,800 gram brain consists of your intellect (or mind). It, too, is influenced by inherited temperament, accounting for the fact that some people are, by nature, analytical perfectionists, with good retention capabilities, while others are prone to be goal-oriented people lovers, with a tendency to find organization and concentration difficult.

We use a file cabinet to symbolize the mind because it is the

principal place of memory. From its file you make your deductions, judgments, and decisions.

Your mind has phenomenal potential, which is almost beyond belief. Scientists inform us that the average person uses only 10 percent of his mind's capabilities during his entire lifetime. If that is true, then most people must die with 10 to 11 billion brain cells still unused.

The vast majority of data concerning the mind has been discovered during the past 100 years, yet the greatest discoveries, scientists anticipate, will surface in the future. The mind's chief function is that of memory, but it also houses our intuition, conscience, sexuality, and many other things. Recent studies indicate a difference between the brains of men and women, attributing some validity to the traditional observation that they think differently. For example, boys and girls from primitive cultures, unfamiliar with modern toys when introduced to them, responded differently. The boys gravitated to trucks and soldier toys, while the girls were drawn to dishes and dolls.

When it comes to learning, the conscious mind, subconscious mind, and imagination are the brain's most significant areas. Apparently everything we see, hear, touch, and smell is recorded on the lobes of our brain, never to be forgotten. Some information, however, remains in our subconscious files and cannot be recalled at will, as can that in the conscious section. That explains why we cannot remember an answer when taking an examination, but before getting home, our eyes may see something that triggers a thought that opens a certain file, causing us to "remember."

We use a file cabinet, rather than a modern computer to symbolize the mind, because it is easier for everyone to understand how it influences feelings, actions, and will. As we have

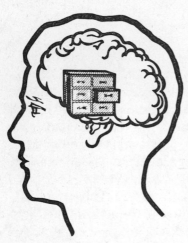

seen, the two primary means of communicating to your brain are through the eyes and ears. It is difficult to exaggerate the importance of using these receptors properly, for how you employ them largely determines how you think (your philosophy of life). And be sure of this: Your philosophy of life will determine the way you live. Actually, your philosophy is the result of your inherited mind, your training, plus what you have seen, read, done, and heard to this point in your life. Whether we call it a world view or the way you look at life, nothing but life itself is more important to you than this philosophical position.

Your inherited temperament also has a significant influence on your personality, helping to determine the way you do things. For example, if you are an introvert, it is because you were born with an introvert temperament; although you can become more aggressive than your natural inclinations suggest, you will never be a spontaneous extrovert. However, your philosophy of life, which you adopt on the basis of what you have programmed into your mind through your eyes and ears, determines the way you look at life; and that will affect your morals, work drive, integrity, and life investment.

Scientists tell us that the brain is our most important organ because it determines the function of our other organs, such as the pituitary, hypothalamus, heart, nervous system, and so forth. We have little control over the involuntary function of the brain, except to provide it good nutrition (both physically and mentally) upon which to operate. The voluntary part of the brain we do control, however, and that largely consists of the three areas we have discussed:

WHAT WE SEE   WHAT WE HEAR   HOW WE THINK

Ever since God first spoke to Adam and Eve, explaining to them how to think, so they would know how to live successful and happy lives, there has been a consistent battle over who will control the thought processes of man's mind—man or God. Sooner or later, every human being makes that decision, and the result is his philosophy of life. Until this generation, parents were the most influential force in helping a child formulate his philosophy. That is no longer true. Modern technology has found ingenious ways to assault the mind of man and child with incredibly beautiful sounds, colors, and visual imagery. Millions of parents have already lost their children's minds to rock stars, atheistic-humanistic educators, sensual entertainers, and a host of other anti-God, amoral, antiman influences.

Since you are what you think, your thought processes today are largely the result of the input that has come to your mind via your eyes and ears. If you are not careful, you will lose the battle for control of your mind and the minds of your children.

Emotional Center

The second significant part of your brain is your heart, or, as scientists call it, your emotional center. This seat of your emotions is located behind your forehead and between your temples. Rather than being heart shaped, as romantics tend to visualize it, in reality it is walnut shaped. Tied neurologically to every organ of your body, it is known as the motor of the body, for it activates both feeling and movement. If your emotional center is disturbed, you will be upset all over. Emotionally induced illness, which according to doctors accounts for 65 to 80 percent of all modern sickness, originates in the emotions. A person who feels angry, fearful, or tense will suffer all kinds of physical ailments, from high blood pressure and ulcers to strokes and brain damage. One doctor has listed 51 diseases that can be incurred this way.

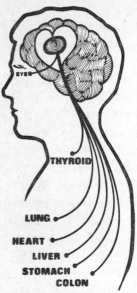

The emotional center is influenced by many factors, beginning with your inherited temperament. That explains why some people are excitable by nature, while others are passive or indifferent. After that, life's experiences, education, beliefs, and most significantly, the mind, influence how we feel.

To illustrate the relationship of the mind to the emotions, visualize a man who owns 2,000 shares of AT&T at $1,000 a share. As he reads his morning paper and finds that one share has dropped to $10, how does he feel? He feels angry, depressed—even suicidal. As soon as his mind comprehended the loss of a fortune, it affected his "heart," or his emotions. Now visualize the same man as he calls his broker and discovers that the newspaper had made a typographical error. A smile brightens his face, and he *feels* relieved. The mind is to the emotions what food is to the body.

For that reason, what the mind feeds upon becomes the most influential force in your life!

One of the great myths of our times is that feelings are spontaneous. Actually, they are created by what you put into your mind. Computer people repeatedly warn, "You get out of a computer only what you program into it," or, more crudely stated, "Garbage in—garbage out." The same can be said for the mind. Whatever the eyes and ears communicate, the mind in turn dispenses. The other senses—smell, taste, and touch—influence our thinking but do not have as significant an impact on our mind.

Consider the unmarried, twenty-one-year-old college student who acknowledged a serious problem with sexual thoughts. Realizing that he was at the zenith of his sex drive, I was not surprised by his confession. In an attempt to help him learn to control his emotional passions, I asked, "What have you been reading and seeing lately?" After skirmishing a bit with vague references to newspapers and magazines, he finally acknowledged a more-than-passing acquaintance with *Playboy* and certain pornographic books. When pressed about movies, he admitted that he had been watching X-rated movies on cable TV. I pointed out to him that such a large intake of pornography was like pouring gasoline on a fire.

The old truism, "You are what you read," could be enlarged to, "You are what you see." What the eyes feast upon forms an impression on the mind, which in turn feeds the emotions. Just as drugs or alcohol influence thoughts and feelings physically, what we see and hear affect our thoughts and emotions.

There is growing evidence today that our warnings to civil leaders a few years ago—that overturning the moral laws upon which this country was built would increase crimes of sex and violence—were fully warranted. In the name of free speech and freedom of the press, we have polluted the minds of our young with pornography, until crime and sexual assaults are now commonplace. The problem will not diminish until we elect public officials with sufficient moral sanity to pass laws prohibiting the distribution of corrupting materials.

Not only are just our morally minded citizens concerned. A recent demonstration of feminists in New York highlighted their concern that the widespread use of "porno" is a threat to them, for they become the victims of rape and assaults.

Sociologist Marvin Wolfgang has stated, "The weight of evidence now suggests that the portrayal of violence tends to encourage the use of physical aggression among people who are exposed to it."[2] Of course it does. Whatever you see or hear influences your mind, which in turn affects your feelings and your emotional center. Feelings, then, are aroused as much by what you see and hear as by who and what you are. If you want the right feelings, see and hear the right things, so you can generate the right thoughts.

Thousands of minors have been taken into custody for crimes that never would have been committed, had it not been for the abuse of porno. I visited a sixteen-year-old in juvenile hall, after he had committed a sex crime that startled everyone who knew him. In checking his room, we found two-thirds of a drawer filled with pornographic filth. It was easy to understand how this lad brought disgrace upon his family and shame to himself. At a time when he was beginning to experience new sexual passions, he *artificially* fanned them by the misuse of his eyes, until his emotions were ignited beyond control. He will probably be haunted by that evil action the rest of his life.

However, that boy was not abnormal. He simply underwent a natural reaction to an abnormal stimulus. Pornography is abnormal! Our youth seem obsessed with sex because depraved adults are providing them the pornographic fuel with which they are burning up their lives.

Admittedly, all visual filth, whether in TV, movies, or books, does not result in crimes of violence. But my counseling experience indicates that it frequently occasions an equally negative effect: reducing the beautiful expression of love in marriage to a sexual expression of passion. In fact, pornography is one of the leading causes of our skyrocketing divorce rate.

Pornography, of course, is not the only phenomenon that influences the emotions. I use it as a graphic illustration pointing up that what you see and hear largely influence how you think, and how you think influences your feelings.

Here is a healthy rule of thumb to follow, when you recognize wrong or harmful feelings: Examine what you have been seeing and hearing lately and how your mind has been thinking. Feelings are not spontaneous; to control them, you must first control your mind.

The Human Will

The third characteristic of the brain, which makes mankind unique from all other living creatures, is the will. No one

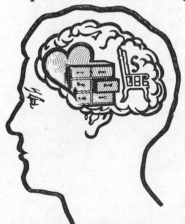

knows where it is located, but we suspect it resides in the brain, because it is so dependent on the mind and emotions. Besides, many dying people have manifested a strong will long after every other bodily function has terminated; when the brain ceased to function, the will vanished.

Like the heart and mind, the will is influenced by a person's inherited temperament, which explains why some people have a weak will, while others by nature are strong willed. After that, the will is influenced by parental training, education, life experiences, what a person reads, sees, and hears, and the way in which he thinks and feels.

Someone has said that whenever the emotions and the will are in conflict, the emotions win. That is usually true, particularly if a person's thoughts are permitted to inflame the feelings for a long enough period of time. A friend of mine is an alcoholic, but for six years he had not touched a drop. One hot day, an urgent thought flashed upon the screen of his imagination: *An ice-cold glass of beer sure would taste good right now.* His conscious mind responded, *Don't do it! You're an alcoholic.* However, because his imagination was visualizing the beer in three-dimensional color, he talked himself into the assurance that, after six years, he had learned to control his problem. Within two hours, he visited a bar, tried one drink, then another—and you can imagine the rest.

The importance of the will should never be underestimated, for both a man's life and his eternity are determined by it. If, for example, he chooses to rebel against God and man, his life will constantly be in turmoil. If, however, he surrenders the control of his life to God and those in rightful authority over him, he will enjoy a life of fulfillment and oneness with both God and his fellowman.

One reason I am alarmed at the current trend that emphasizes children's rights, at the expense of parental rights, is that this will inhibit parents from administering loving discipline to their children. Consequently, the child will grow up without self-control and may rebel against the laws of God and society. Such rebels are vulnerable subjects for the self-centered philosophy found in humanistic education, movies, books, and so forth.

Of the three interdependent areas of the human brain, the mind is by far the most significant, for it ultimately determines both our feelings and the strength and direction of our will. That is why I call this book *The Battle for the Mind.* The principal struggle of life is to determine who will control man's mind.

Good or Evil

As far back as we can go in recorded history, we find that man has always been aware that life was a battle between good and evil. Thirty-five hundred years ago, evil was termed "The way of man," or, "The way that seemed right to man." The good way has always been called "God's way." These two avenues of life are really philosophies of life dictating how a person lives.

The apostle Paul was aware of that difference when he wrote his classic words to Corinth, Greece, where much of our modern humanistic thinking originated (1 Corinthians 1:17–25):

> For Christ sent me not to baptize, but to preach the gospel: not with wisdom of words, lest the cross of Christ should be made of none effect. For the preaching of the cross is to them that perish foolishness; but unto us which are saved it is the power of God. For it is written, I will destroy the wisdom of the wise, and will bring to nothing the understanding of the prudent. Where is the wise? where is the scribe? where is the disputer of this world? hath not God made foolish the wisdom of this world? For after that in the wisdom of God the world by wisdom knew not God, it pleased God by the foolishness of preaching to save them that believe. For the Jews require a sign, and the Greeks seek after wisdom: But we preach Christ crucified, unto the Jews a stumblingblock, and unto the Greeks foolishness; But unto them which are called, both Jews and Greeks, Christ the power of God, and the wisdom of God. Because the foolishness of God is wiser than men; and the weakness of God is stronger than men.

This passage of divine revelation delineates two opposing lines of reasoning: man's wisdom and God's wisdom. Paul showed the Greeks, who in his day were the ultimate in intellectualism and philosophy, that man's wisdom was inherently wrong. He called it "foolishness" (or futility). By contrast, the wisdom of God is called "power!" That is, it possesses the energy to produce the happiness, fulfillment, and meaning to which all men aspire. These are not available through man's wisdom, but only through God's.

The fifty-year-old head of a university science department in our city accepted Christ through the faithful witness of his wife and family. Several months after his conversion, this man, a Ph.D. for many years, exclaimed, "I can hardly believe I could be so dumb for so long! I thought I knew something before I was converted, but the greatest period of learning in my life has taken place these past few months." He was not dumb— just overly educated in man's wisdom, to the exclusion of God's wisdom. There are millions like him today. In fact, the battle for the mind that is raging presently is similar to what it was in Paul's day. Our generation speaks of humanism versus biblical truth, but it is the same battle between good and evil.

More people (including Christians) are adversely affected by humanism than they realize. It is the dominant philosophy of life in the Western world, having captured secular education, TV, publications, movies, and radio. Sometimes it appears omnipresent. Every citizen of Western culture should understand and expose humanism for the philosophical "foolishness" it represents. For that reason, we shall dedicate an entire chapter to man's wisdom, or the humanist man. First, however, we need to determine humanism's origin.

2

Humanizing America

During the last 200 years, humanism (man's wisdom) has captivated the thinking of the Western world. After conquer-

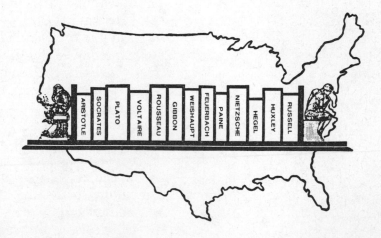

ing Europe's colleges and universities, it spread to America, where it has developed a stranglehold on all public education. Recognizing as they did the strategic nature of both education and the communications field in waging their battle for the minds of mankind, the humanists gradually moved in, until they virtually controlled both. Almost every major magazine, newspaper, TV network, secular book publisher, and movie producer is a committed humanist, surrounding himself with editors and newscasters who share his philosophy and seldom permit anything to be presented that contradicts humanism, unless forced to by community pressure.

Humanism seems so credible and logical to the man who does not understand God's wisdom that it is adopted readily by the masses—much to their own peril. Today's wave of crime and violence in our streets, promiscuity, divorce, shattered dreams, and broken hearts can be laid right at the door of secular humanism. As the Scriptures teach, "Professing themselves to be wise, they became fools" (Romans 1:22). Unless our nation's leaders and a sufficient number of American citizens become aware of the truth about humanism, it will ultimately lead to anarchy, and our culture will be destroyed. Dr. Francis Schaeffer has warned that the ultimate end of humanism is always chaos.

Simply defined, humanism is man's attempt to solve his problems independently of God. Since moral conditions have become worse and worse in direct proportion to humanism's influence, which has moved our country from a biblically based society to an amoral, "democratic" society during the past forty years, one would think that humanists would realize the futility of their position. To the contrary, they treacherously refuse to face the reality of their failures, blaming them instead on traditional religion or ignorance or capitalism or religious superstitions.

An obvious example of the futility of humanistic thinking appears in the United Nations. Thirty-five years ago, the world's humanists—who founded the UN and exercise absolute control over it—promised that the UN would solve the problem of war and be the means of ushering in world peace. How well has the UN fulfilled that pledge? We have had more wars, deaths, and international catastrophes during these thirty-five years than in any comparable period in world history. If you doubt that statement, just ask what the UN has done to help the Cambodians, South Vietnamese boat people, Angolans, Ugandans, and the twenty-five countries of Africa under totalitarian dictatorships. The world has put billions of dollars at the disposal of these humanist world planners, who repay their supporters with increased dividends of futility.

I did not have to be a prophet in 1945, when the UN was founded to predict it would never meet its goals, for our Lord warned mankind, "Without Me, you can do nothing." The year 1945 was the year the humanists decided to exclude God from the UN, to keep from offending the Communists.

Another illustration of humanistic futility can be found in the prophecy of Dr. Horace Mann, who probably did more to humanize the American school system than any other person. In 1850, he sold America on the idea that secular education would solve the problems of crime and poverty in 100 years. I'll let you be the judge of whether that is true—even though we will spend 140 billion dollars on secular humanistic education this year.

The Roots of Humanism

Humanism is a man-centered philosophy that attempts to solve the problems of man and the world independently of God.

The wisdom of man, often called secular humanism today, can be traced back to the rudimentary writings of man. In fact, only two lines of reasoning permeate all of literature: biblical revelation (the wisdom of God) and the wisdom of man. All books are based either on man's thoughts or God's thoughts. For a teacher to influence succeeding generations, he must either reproduce his philosophy in written form or inspire his disciples to pen his thoughts. Thus the philosophers who have

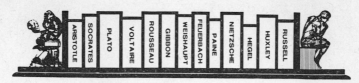

had the greatest impact on the minds of our young were writers. Name a well-known philosopher, and you have named a writer.

The Greek thinkers were the first to systematically lay out the philosophy of humanism that Paul described as the wisdom of man. It was based on two of Protagoras's fifth century B.C. misconceptions: "Man is the measure of all things" and "Contradictory assertions are equally true." These humanistic concepts have been amplified through the years by scores of atheists, until today they have formed a well-defined system of thought that contradicts almost every basic concept of biblical revelation. The prophet Isaiah was accurate when he showed man's wisdom to be 180 degrees in opposition to God's wisdom: "For my thoughts are not your thoughts, neither are your ways my ways, saith the Lord" (Isaiah 55:8).

The humanistic philosophy of the Greeks almost perished with the destruction of their country by the Romans. Unfortunately for history, the Romans were not given to much original thought, so they adopted the philosophy, art, architecture, and social customs of Greece, merged them with their own, and propagated Hellenistic culture throughout the Roman world. Somehow they preserved the writings of the Greeks, in spite of the spread of Christianity during the early centuries after Christ.

However, so effective did Christianity become in influencing the thought of Western man for over 1,200 years that, from the death of Christ until the twelfth century, little humanistic thinking is found. Most of the colleges and universities of Europe were dominated by Catholic thought.

Interestingly enough, one of the most important thinkers helping to lay the foundation for modern humanism was a dedicated Dominican, later sainted, named Thomas Aquinas (1225–1274).

> He was the outstanding theologian of his day and his thinking is still dominant in some circles of the Roman Catholic Church. . . . Aquinas held that man had revolted against God and thus was fallen, but Aquinas had an incomplete view of the Fall. He thought that the Fall did not affect man as a whole but only in part. In his view the will was fallen or corrupted but the intellect was not affected. Thus people could rely on their own human wisdom, and this meant that people were free to mix the teachings of the Bible with the teachings of the non-Christian philosophers. . . .[3]
>
> Among the Greek philosophers, Thomas Aquinas relied especially on one of the greatest, Aristotle (384–322 B.C.). . . . Aquinas managed to have Aristotle accepted, so the ancient non-Christian philosophy was reenthroned.[4]

From this we see that Western man's philosophic romance with human wisdom began in the medieval period, with Aquinas. It is an irony of history that a man who was sainted by his church as a scholar was responsible for reviving an almost dead philosophy, which has become the most dangerous religion in the world today—humanism.

By raising human wisdom to a level that gave it equal weight with biblical revelation, Aquinas opened the door for freethinking educators to gradually implant more of the wisdom of man, as they discarded the wisdom of God. Eventually man's wisdom became truth to secular man, and God's wisdom became error. That explains why today's humanists, who grandly proclaim their tolerance of opposing views and proudly advocate respect for the opinions of others, become so vicious in their expressed hatred of Christianity and its absolutes. To humanists, Christian thought is a mortal foe. They often become obsessed with the idea that they render a service for humanity by stamping out Christianity, forcing its exclusion from public education, and blocking every biblical moral principle they can. Because the biblical revelation and moral absolutes of Christianity comprise "public enemy number one," they work relentlessly for their destruction.

The Renaissance gave birth to modern humanism. Upon the foundation laid by Aquinas, considered by many humanists the most influential thinker in history, additional building blocks of man's wisdom were added to "Thus saith the Lord God." Gradually the focus of education shifted from God to "Man, the measure of all things," who eventually was deemed autonomous and independent of God. This freed man from absolutes and permitted him to be the God, or judge, of his own behavior.

Florence, Italy, became the cultural headquarters of the Renaissance. The glorification of mankind, particularly in his human form, was soon reflected in art. The giant replica of Michelangelo's magnificent David stands nude, overlooking that beautiful city. Quite naturally, this contradicts the wisdom of God, for early in Genesis, the Creator followed man's folly by giving him animal skins to cover his nakedness. Ever since, there has been a conflict concerning clothes, with man demanding the freedom to go naked. The Renaissance obsession with nude "art forms" was the forerunner of the modern humanist's demand for pornography in the name of freedom. Both resulted in a self-destructive lowering of moral standards. Dr. Schaeffer highlights this fallacy of the wisdom of man when he notes, "The most important individual thing for man is man himself" and, "Beginning from man alone, Renaissance humanism—and humanism ever since—has found no way to arrive at universals or absolutes which give meaning to existence and morals."[5]

French Skepticism and Modern Humanism

The two men who wield the greatest influence upon the humanistic ideals, morals, and philosophy of today's college students are the French skeptics Voltaire and Rousseau. Both were trained in Jesuit colleges, yet both rejected anything supernatural and adopted an ethically amoral code.

Voltaire's skepticism is a classic example of the danger of providing the wrong kind of teacher for a child. Because he was obviously endowed with a superior mind, his parents hired a tutor, "a dissolute abbé who taught him skepticism along with his prayers."[6] With his skepticism well entrenched prior to his college days, it is no wonder that he rejected Christianity and became antagonistic to the faith of his parents. Faith and skepticism are like sunglasses: They color the way a person looks at all things, particularly revelation and the supernatural.

Voltaire, often called "the father of the Enlightenment," was really the logical (if you can call a philosophy that always produces chaos "logical") result of Renaissance (rebirth of Greek humanism) thinking.

> The utopian dream of the Enlightenment can be summed up by five words: reason, nature, happiness, progress, and liberty. It was thoroughly secular in its thinking. The humanistic elements which had risen during the Renaissance came to flood tide in the Enlightenment. Here was man starting from himself absolutely. And if the humanistic elements of the Renaissance stand in sharp contrast to the Reformation, the Enlightenment was in total antithesis to it. The two stood for and were based upon absolutely different things in an absolute way, and they produced absolutely different results.[7]

A popular misconception suggests that only the "common" man, or one of mediocre intelligence, finds faith acceptable. Historically, that just is not true! Some of the most brilliant, well-educated people were and are men and women of faith.

Skepticism is not innate; it has to be taught, either verbally or through the printed page. Before the age of Voltaire and Rousseau, we can point to numerous men of faith with intelligence equaling that of the famous skeptics. Consider such names as John Wycliffe (1320-1384), Martin Luther (1483-1546), John Calvin (1509-1564), Sir Isaac Newton (1642-1727), or Jonathan Edwards (1703-1758). These men of faith were also thinkers and writers, but the skeptics either refused to read these men or perused their works through the glasses of skepticism, which filtered all religious precepts through the naturalistic lenses of deism.

In June 1789, the first phase of the liberal bourgeois plan of the French Revolution was at its height.... Here the members of the National Assembly swore to establish a constitution. Their base, consciously, was purely a humanist theory of rights. On August 26, 1789, they issued the Declaration of the Rights of Man. It sounded fine, but it had nothing to rest upon. In the Declaration of the Rights of Man what was called "the Supreme Being" equaled "the sovereignty of the nation"—that is, the general will of the people. Not only was there a contrast to England's Bloodless Revolution, but a sharp contrast with what resulted in the United States from the Declaration of Independence which was made thirteen years earlier. One had the Reformation base, the other did not.

It took two years for the National Constituent Assembly to draft a constitution (1789-1791). Within a year it was a dead letter. By that time what is often known as the Second French Revolution was in motion, leading to a bloodbath that ended with the revolutionary leaders themselves being killed.

To make their outlook clear, the French changed the calendar and called 1792 the "year one," and destroyed many of the things of the past, even suggesting the destruction of the cathedral at Chartres. They proclaimed the goddess of Reason in Notre-Dame Cathedral in Paris and in other churches in France, including Chartres. In Paris, the goddess was personified by an actress, Demoiselle Candeille, carried shoulder-high into the cathedral by men dressed in Roman costumes.

Like the humanists of the Renaissance, the men of the Enlightenment pushed aside the Christian base and heritage and looked back to the old pre-Christian times. In Voltaire's home in Ferney the picture he hung (in such a way on the wall at the foot of his bed that it was the first thing he saw each day) was a painting of the goddess Diana with a small new crescent moon on her head and a very large one under her feet. She is reaching down to help men.

How quickly all the humanist ideals came to grief! In September 1792 began the massacre in which some 1,300 prisoners were killed. Before it was all over, the government and its agents killed 40,000 people, many of them peasants. Maximilien Robespierre (1758–1794), the revolutionary leader, was himself executed in July 1794. This destruction came not from outside the system; it was produced by the system. As in the later Russian Revolution the revolutionaries on their humanist base had only two options—anarchy or repression.[8]

Humanism's Incurable Optimism

We would expect true thinkers to profit by their mistakes, even in the field of philosophy. But such is not the case. In view of the total failure of Enlightenment humanism to produce reason, liberty, freedom, and progress through the French and Russian revolutions, and in light of the chaos, suffering, and totalitarian repression they instituted—which is the ultimate consequence of no absolutes—one would hope that the humanist mind would become suspicious that perhaps man without law really can't be trusted. But those historic lessons were lost on the humanist mind.*

---

* Humanism appeals to the intellect, and intelligent people tend to be largely of the Melancholy temperament. Although endowed with great talent and creativity (the world's foremost artists, musicians, sculptors, scholars, philos-

Instead of recognizing that elimination of absolutes always produces chaos, followed by repression, the humanists of the Enlightenment decided they had acted in haste. As a result, they established a two-pronged attack on man's mind, through books and education. Ironically, they utilized the most significant invention of the fifteenth century, the printing press, whose first accomplishment was the printing of the Bible in 1451. This amazing machine and the new translations of Scripture contributed greatly to the Reformation in northern Europe and England, enabling the common man to read God's revelation in his own language for the first time. In addition, Calvin, Luther, and other scholarly reformers, all of them voluminous writers, had likewise used the printed page to explain the wisdom of God to the people.

Unfortunately, Enlightenment humanists knew that the battle for control of man's mind would be won or lost largely through reading and education, so they, too, began to communicate their philosophies through art, fiction, plays, poetry, and teaching. Voltaire alone produced eighty-three volumes of books, pamphlets, and plays that swept through France and southern Europe. Since some of the northern kings forbade the distribution of certain Enlightenment writings because of their poisonous humanism, their spread was somewhat checked until the eighteenth and nineteenth centuries.

The colleges and universities of Europe, supported by kings (with the tax money forceably seized from the workingman), became the ideal transmission belt for "enlightened" human-

---

ophers, and educators have been predominantly of the Melancholy temperament), Melancholies are apt to be idealistic, theoretical and impractical, making them vulnerable to humanistic philosophy, even though it has a long history of disorder, anguish, and despair. For a description of temperament and its influence on a person's thinking, see one of the author's three books on temperament: *Spirit-Controlled Temperament, Transformed Temperaments,* and *Understanding the Male Temperament.*

ism. Universal education was unknown, and thus only the bright, gifted young people, the sons of politicians or the rich, could gain a higher education. Gradually the humanists literally took over most of the colleges and universities of the continent and became the high priests of education. With missionary zeal, they taught their philosophic prejudices of "No God—no absolutes—self-sufficient and self-indulgent man," much to the consternation of the students' parents.

As technology increased, so did self-government, and almost every country in Europe began to multiply its number of government officials. Where did these bureaucrats receive their education? In humanistic colleges and universities. It is no wonder that government and education have historically worked in concert, much to the bewilderment of the noneducated workingman. His taxes have paid the salaries of his government and educational overlords, but they have been traditionally unresponsive to his needs or desires. The only reason Western man has not been totally enslaved by these high priests of the wisdom of man is that the church has taught, written, and communicated the wisdom of God to a sufficient number of people.

Wherever possible, Christian schools, Bible societies, and Christian publishers have valiantly fought the battle for control of the mind—a battle that they are losing today.

America's Worldwide Influence

At the risk of being accused of nationalistic pride, I would point out that, had it not been for the Christian influence in America, our contemporary world would have completely lost the battle for the mind and would doubtless live in a totalitarian, one-world, humanistic state. England saved Europe from Napoleon in the first quarter of the nineteenth century, but by the twentieth century, she had so lost her biblical, Reformation base of thought that she needed the assistance of America to overthrow Germany's Kaiser Wilhelm and Adolf Hitler, both of whom would have imposed a humanistic totalitarianism upon Europe, if they had won either war.

The eighteenth-century Enlightenment produced some of the greatest philosophical evils in the history of mankind. From its fountainhead have flowed atheism, rationalism, illuminism, socialism, Communism, evolution, Freudianism, behaviorism, and ultimately the doomsday philosophy of existentialism. So powerfully did existential thought permeate education and government in Europe before the turn of the century that, according to Dr. Schaeffer, Europe crossed what he calls "the line of despair" around 1880. He estimates that, because of her stronger biblical base of thought, America did not cross that line until the 1930s. Since then, humanism has run rampant in our public educational system, until today it has swallowed up official government thinking, the media, and virtually every area of communication except church-related ministries and education.

With the increase of humanistic thinking in America has come a relentless expansion in government. In 1920 there was approximately one government employee for every 100 citizens. Today one out of six Americans works for either the local, state, or federal government.

The establishment of big government has propagated such loss of freedom that many knowledgeable people fear we will lose our traditional freedoms before the year 2,000. Only when enough morally minded voters recognize that humanists are not qualified to hold public office or to receive taxpayer support for brainwashing their children under the guise of public education, will they vote in pro-moral leaders who will return our country to the biblical base upon which it was founded. Then we can once again enjoy a morally sane society.

The Greatness of America

Volumes have been written on the secret of America's greatness. Many Christians mistakenly presume that since our country was founded as a Christian nation, it has enjoyed the blessings of God. Historically, that is not true. This country was founded on a basic consensus of Christian principles—more so than any nation in history—but even that is not the whole story. Having pondered the greatness of our land, I would love to say that our many churches and their humanitarian concerns and soul-winning endeavors have given us the greatest degree of freedom, liberty, and prosperity that any nation has enjoyed since the days when Solomon was king of Israel. Unfortunately, that would not be true.

We cannot claim the world's largest land surface, for Brazil, Australia, China, and Russia are larger. It isn't that we have the world's greatest natural resources, for Zimbabwe, Rhodesia, is naturally richer, as are South Africa and Brazil. It isn't our unique nationality, for we are a melting pot of people largely from Europe but more recently from Africa, Mexico, and other places.

In truth, what has granted more freedom for the longest period of time (over 200 years of self-government is an all-time world record) to the largest number of people, while at the same time producing the greatest wealth for the most people, can be traced to the two distinctives that are presently in great jeopardy: our Bible-based form of government and our unique Bible-based educational system.

Our Bible-Based Form of Government

It is improper to say that America was founded on Christian principles, for that would unnecessarily exclude the Jewish community. America was founded on biblical principles, all of

which are found in the Old Testament and therefore should
not exclude any but the most anti-God, antimoral humanist
thinkers of our day. As we shall see in a later chapter, such
thinkers comprise scarcely 4 percent of our nation's population.

Admittedly, many considered America a Christian nation,
until the humanists took over the major spheres of influence
forty years ago and began to change all of our time-honored
moral values. Attorney John Whitehead cites some interesting
sources confirming that many influential people thought this
nation was founded as a Christian country:

> In 1892 the United States Supreme Court made an exhaus-
> tive study of the supposed connection between Christianity
> and the government of the United States. After reviewing hun-
> dreds of volumes of historical documents, the Court asserted,
> "These references ... add a volume of unofficial declarations
> to the mass of organic utterances that this is a religious people
> ... a Christian nation." Likewise, in 1931 Supreme Court Jus-
> tice George Sutherland reviewed the 1892 decision in refer-
> ence to another case and reiterated that Americans are a
> "Christian people." And in 1952 Justice William O. Douglas
> affirmed that "we are a religious people and our institutions
> presuppose a Supreme Being."[9]

The Christian consensus that Dr. Schaeffer postulates is the
best way to describe the philosophical thought in early
America. It certainly did not originate here. Most colonists
were Englishmen, and almost all were Europeans, who
brought to the New World a Reformation mental attitude.
Some, it is true, introduced the Enlightenment heresies of Voltaire, Rousseau, and others, but these did not predominate.
Therefore, our government of law was based on a respect and
reverence for God and the realization that man was His special
creation. Such expressions as "Divine Providence" and "nature and Nature's God" appear in the Declaration of Indepen-

dence as the source of man's inalienable rights. (By contrast, humanism contends that man and the state are the sources from which man's human rights originate.) The last six commandments of the Decalogue, dealing with man's treatment of his fellowman, and the civil laws of the Old Testament formed the basis for our laws and our Constitution.

As Dr. Schaeffer points out, a government based on biblical principles, particularly as shaped through Reformation thinking, was not perfect, but it "gave society the opportunity for tremendous freedom, but without chaos."[10] Our unique check-and-balance system of government would never have been conceived by humanism. It is borrowed directly from Scripture.

Today the humanists ridicule the Puritan work ethic, free enterprise, private ownership of land, and capitalism—even though these concepts, which emanated from biblical teaching, have produced the greatest good for the largest number of people in history. We discard them at our national peril, for a free and healthy economy thrives best on a moral foundation that engenders trust and faith in one's fellowman. Because of the biblical base of most Americans' thinking, this faith was common as our laws were formulated.

In *The Reconstruction of the Republic,* Dr. Harold O. J. Brown underscores that fact when he claims:

> ... the Bible has had a tremendous formative influence on people and institutions even when it has not been accepted as the authoritative Word of God. It is perfectly correct to say that a substantial measure of American culture, attitudes, literary style, even language and laws and political institutions is biblical in origin and inspiration.
>
> What is the practical meaning of this identifiably biblical heritage? It is very simple, and amazingly important. The basic source of values in American society is biblical. An important secondary source, as we shall see, lies in a nonbiblical philo-

sophical humanism. Neither of these, and particularly the biblical source, which is the more pervasive, can be removed from American society without removing the heart from our value-system and civilization.[11]

The United States Constitution, Brown explains:

> ... is an instrument whereby fundamental values can be protected, defining the procedures, principles, and methods whereby government can function to allow the people to give content to their lives. But the Constitution itself cannot give that content. In the early days, no one supposed that it would. There was a sufficiently clear value-consensus among Americans so that, while degrees of commitment or differences of emphasis existed, there was little doubt as to the fundamental nature of good and evil, or virtue and vice.[12]

The Constitution was designed "to create a framework for the preservation of values that the people acknowledge to be right and good, not to create those values."[13]

Our Bible-Based School System

Until a few years ago, America led the world in providing its citizens with the greatest educational system. We were the first nation to insure compulsory education, enabling even the poorest of children to learn to read and write. Our nation's amazing industrialization and mechanization were largely due to the high degree of education among our people. Have you ever wondered where this came from? It certainly did not reflect the Virginia colonial system, where the education of the young was entirely dependent on the financial ability of the parents, as it had been in Europe.

The New England colonies and Pennsylvania (under Governor William Penn) were the originators of the idea that every household should seek to educate its children. And we must not forget the motivation of godly Puritans and Pilgrims, who lived during the great age of biblical translation, making it possible for the common people to read God's Word for themselves. That was a monumental time in English history. Consequently, the New World settlers not only quested for religious freedom but carried a burning desire that their children be able to read the Bible for themselves.

Among the early settlers, of course, were ministers of the Gospel, who located churches in the heart of the new communities as they sprang up. Since the minister was one of the few educated people in the community, and because he had to work to supplement his small salary (usually by farming), the town settlers often engaged him as the teacher of their young. In exchange, the other settlers did his farming. The term *one-room schoolhouse* is more than a cliché in American history; that one-room building not only accommodated all the grades, first through sixth or eighth, Monday through Friday, but it housed the church and its activities on Sundays.

It would be impossible to overestimate the profound moral influence of the churches on the young and on education during the seventeenth and eighteenth centuries. First graders didn't learn to read with "See Jane run" or "Jump, Spot, jump," as they do today. Instead, the man of God would normally start them out with, "In the beginning, God created the heavens and the earth." The *McGuffey Reader*—often ridiculed by today's humanistic educators, who are doing such a disastrous job of teaching Johnnie to read—would tell the first grader, "God made the world and all things in it." The text was filled with references to God, obedience, morality, and character building. Such moral character training of our young is absolutely essential to the maintenance of a morally sane and safe society. As one European statesman observed after visiting America over fifty years ago, "America is great because she is

good. If she ever ceases to be good, she will cease being great."
Moral goodness has to be taught clearly and consistently to our
young, because mankind is not good by nature.

As the young nation matured and its cities grew in population, the ministry demanded all of the pastor's time. Schoolteachers were trained to take the minister's place in the classroom, but even they reflected the biblical consensus of thought,
because of the profound influence of the church on education.
In 1636, Harvard College was founded by Reverend John
Harvard, who contributed the land and his own private library.
On the gateposts today appears an inscription that explains
why he established the school: to maintain "A Literate
Clergy." John Harvard recognized that only a handful of ministers from England would be willing to migrate to this new
and rough land, so he was burdened to start a Christian college
in America. For many years, Harvard College was the principal educational-training center for ministers and missionaries,
as well as schoolteachers. Since then, hundreds of ministers
have founded Christian colleges, Bible schools, graduate
schools, universities, and seminaries. For the first 100 years of
American history, every college started in this country was
founded by a church, denomination, or religious group.
American education was never intended to be godless.

It is estimated that for over 250 years of our history, Harvard, Princeton, and Yale were the primary teacher-training
centers. Although each had a different denominational origin,
together they shared a common goal: to prepare ministers and
missionaries to preach the Gospel. Educating teachers for the
growing schools in America was a natural outgrowth of that
vision.

Teachers trained in these schools understandably reflected
the biblical moral values of their respective colleges. Consequently, public education, though never intended to be a
source of evangelism, was highly flavored with biblical morals

and formulated the greatest mass-character-building program in the history of the world. The biblical influence of the nineteenth century public schools is evidenced by the fact that the Catholic parochial schools were started, according to one educator, "to keep our Catholic youth out of those Protestant public schools."

Today, public education is so humanistic that it is both anti-Catholic and anti-Protestant—because it is anti-God. With the expulsion of God from the schools, the view that man was created by God and thus responsible for obeying His moral absolutes, deteriorated drastically. As we shall see, the chaos of today's public-education system is in direct proportion to its religious obsession with humanism. And as we have already observed, humanism ultimately destroys everything it touches.

You may well wonder how the world's greatest educational system, based solidly on biblical principles, was taken over by humanism. We answer, "Very gradually!"

The process did not begin with Horace Mann, although he probably did more to humanize American education in the nineteenth century than any other educator, and thus we tend to trace humanistic roots back to him. Mann was vigorously opposed by ministers of his day, who foresaw the shift from a biblical to a humanistic base for education, but their resistance was gradually overcome. During the latter part of the nineteenth century, many of our bright young educators went to Europe to pursue their graduate degrees. They enrolled at the Sorbonne in France, Bonn University in Germany, Edinburgh University in Scotland, Oxford University in England, and many other humanistic graduate schools. In time, these professors returned with their Ph.D.s, bringing with them the skepticism, atheism, rationalism, and existentialism of humanistic Europe.

John Dewey, the most influential educator of the twentieth century, did more for the humanist takeover of American education than anyone else. The leader of the progressive movement in education, Dewey was an atheist and a board member of the American Humanist Association in 1933, when it hammered out the first *Humanist Manifesto*. His experimental and pragmatic theories of education were undergirded by his claim that truth is relative, that absolutes are not admissible, that evolutionary theory is valid. "There is no God and there is no soul," he affirmed.[14]

Dewey viewed traditional education with alarm. When he observed the fixed standards and rules of conduct, the moral training that naturally flowed from these standards, and the sense of conformity that bound so many institutions, he rejected traditionalism and proposed the following:

- Expression and cultivation of individuality (as opposed to imposition from above)
- Free activity (as opposed to external discipline)
- Learning through experience (as opposed to texts and teachers)
- Acquiring skills as a means of attaining ends which have direct vital appeal (as opposed to drill)
- Making the most of the opportunities of present life (as opposed to preparation for a more-or-less remote future)
- Acquaintance with a changing world (as opposed to static aims and materials).[15]

Allowing such principles to be developed by humanists has led to the present predicament of public education. *Free expression of oneself* easily becomes self-addiction and rebellion—the "I demand to do my own thing" syndrome—in opposition to divine control and educational discipline. *Learning through experience* may lead one to trust his limited observations and experiments, rather than be instructed and tempered by history, learned teachers, and Scripture. Focusing upon the now and endeavoring to become *the ideal social man* may supplant one's preparation for eternity. *Learning to cope with a changing world* may be equated with building a house on shifting sands—without foundation, without stability, forever detached from eternal verities.

In *A Common Faith* Dewey gives his main ideas on religion. Essentially religion is an attempt to adjust to the actual situations of life, and these valuable experiences should be emancipated from the historical forms of organized religions which are repellent to the modern mind. Since the situation changes from age to age, religion should also change ... real values shall be divorced from creeds and cults, for these values are not so bound up with any item of intellectual assent such as the existence of God. The details of religion must be sought through the only gateway to knowledge that there is, viz., science.[16]

Attempting to apply the scientific to education, Dewey succeeded in stripping from American education its final vestiges of Christian message and purpose.

The schoolhouse was not a hazardous place to work, back in the days when moral principles and character building were taught along with the basics in education. But federal aid to education, which really started in 1957, began the humanist domination of our schools. Since then, the philosophical control of our schools has passed from local communities to the federal government, for all practical purposes. In order to procure federal aid, schools have to accept federally approved policies that feature humanistic thinking—regardless of community moral standards.

During the past ten or fifteen years, parents and pro-moral citizens have become increasingly alarmed over the atheistic amorality of our schools, until today a coalition of antihumanist pro-moralists is becoming quite vocal and active. Gradually they are coming to realize that a humanist is a humanist is a humanist! That is, he believes as a humanist, thinks as a humanist, acts as a humanist, and makes decisions as a hu-

manist. Whether he is a politician, government official, or educator, he does not think like a pro-moral American, but like a
humanist. Consequently, he is not fit to govern us or to train
our young.

The growing coalition of pro-moral Americans is a sleeping
giant that is gradually awakening to the realization that it has
largely ignored the electoral process for decades. Unless it asserts itself and elects pro-moral people to office, America in the
twenty-first century will be a humanist country, for the morals
and philosophy of the public-school system of today will become the moral philosophy of our nation, in twenty to thirty
years.

As long as biblical thought prevailed in the public-school
system, there was no real need for pro-moral people to put on a
drive to get moralists elected to government office, for the majority of our lawmakers reflected the morals of the people. But
all of that has changed in the last thirty to fifty years. Humanism has surreptitiously commandeered our once-great school
system. It has ingeniously conceived a plan to introduce an inordinate number of humanists into government, where they
continually pass laws that favor the advancement of humanism
and chaos, at the expense of the biblical base for a moral society that produced the liberty, peace, and safety we once enjoyed.

This next decade will be a decade of destiny for America,
which will become increasingly humanistic or Christian in its
philosophy. It will certainly be a decade of exciting challenge
for all those who are committed to Christian absolutes and
biblical principles. The next two chapters will delineate the
basic differences between these two philosophies. Then we will
examine what measures we can take to turn this country from
atheistic humanism and chaos to biblical principles and blessing.

The issue will be decided during the 1980s!

3

The Wisdom of God

My high-school English teacher used to have an interesting way of shocking her lethargic class into alertness. She would

pound on her desk, put her fist under her chin, and challenge
us to "Strike the pose of The Thinker." She repeatedly called
our attention to the Greek athlete, cast in bronze, in front of
the Detroit public library. With muscles bulging, he sat deeply
engrossed in thought.

That thinker, and all like him, could summon every ounce of
psychic energy at his disposal and never come to a realization
of the truth. In fact, today man is farther from the answer to
the questions that have plagued philosophers for centuries
than he was in the days of Greece. Any philosophy text will
show that the major questions of man have universally been:

- Who am I?
- Where did I come from?
- Why am I here?
- Where am I going?
- How can I get there?

Recent surveys taken among college students demonstrate
that these questions continue to perplex the serious student.
Unfortunately, those who seek ultimate answers amid the

writings of men are looking in the wrong place. The wisdom of man cannot produce satisfactory replies to such questions. And we hasten to add that, without appropriate and satisfying answers, our educated populace is not really prepared for life.

The apostle Paul warned the Greek thinkers of his day that "... in the wisdom of God, the world by wisdom did not know God ..." (1 Corinthians 1:21 NKJB-NT). In other words, all the thinkers in the world will never conceive independently the secrets of life, origins, and destiny. No, Paul explained, they come only by revelation. No wonder the thinkers of his day did not know God; they had not accepted the Hebrew law and the prophets. And today nothing has changed! Even though God has given a complete revelation of Himself and the mysteries of life, as recorded in the sixty-six books of the Bible, the intelligentsia largely rejects it.

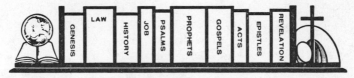

The Bible, which contains that portion of the wisdom of God that He has chosen to share with mankind, not only produces the intellectual base for a morally sane society but gives man clear answers to the major questions of life. These revealed answers cannot be naturally deduced. Consider the following basics, which I shall present briefly.

True Wisdom

God   The Bible presents God as the uncaused Cause of all things, infinite in wisdom, omnipotent, holy in character, yet lovingly interested in every detail of man's life.

That man finds it difficult to conceive of a God so powerful that He could create more universes than man can count, yet is interested in each facet of man's life, does not negate that truth. The problem with such things is that man's finite brain can only conceive a limited God.

Creation   "How did life get here?" The answer to this question appears in the first verse of divine revelation: Genesis 1:1. The details of that creation, found in Genesis 2:1–7, make it clear that the formation of our physical universe was not the result of a lengthy natural process, but an instantaneous act of creation.

Accepting the creation of man by the direct act of God has always been a matter of faith in the revelation of God. Obviously the person who disbelieves in a supernatural God will find it difficult to believe in creation. Today, however, it is easier to believe than it once was, for many men of science have sifted through the evidence and offered scientific documentation for creationism. In fact, one of my colleagues, Dr. Henry M. Morris, is known as "Mr. Creation." This scientist, an educator for 38 years (13 years as the head of the third-largest engineering school in America), who holds a Ph.D. in hydrology from the University of Minnesota, is a prolific writer. He has written a classic engineering textbook currently in use. In 1970, he founded the Institute for Creation Research, which presently employs ten well-known creation scientists. Dr. Morris also served several years as president of over 600 members of the Creation Research Society. Membership of this society is limited to men who hold graduate degrees in science and have signed a statement of their belief in creation. No longer can it be said that men of science and education reject the concept of creation.

Dr. Morris has said, "There is no evidence that vertically-upward evolution is possible, that it ever occurs in the present or that it ever occurred in the past. If one believes in evolution, he must do so by faith, not by observation." The facts of science do not *prove* creation to be true (only the Word of the Creator can do that), but they do advance creationism as a much more effective scientific "model" of origins than evolutionism.

Civil Morality The biblical base of morality is popularly referred to as the Judeo-Christian ethic. That is, Jews and Christians agree on the basic standards of morality upon which this country was founded. These precepts are absolute: not subject to revision or deletion by any earthly potentate or Supreme Court, without resulting in the destruction of society.

Christians and Jews can agree on the civil/

moral code of ethics because it is well-defined in the Old Testament. In fact, no new civil standards are proposed in the New Testament, which addresses itself more to a higher, Christian code of ethics, voluntarily obeyed on an individual basis. The Christian code is so much higher than the Old Testament civil/moral standard that in obeying God, Christians should automatically comply with the moral code of their land.

Biblical civil morals are based on six of the Ten Commandments that refer to man's relationship to his fellowman. Consider:

- Thou shalt not steal.
- Thou shalt not bear false witness.
- Thou shalt not commit murder.
- Thou shalt not commit adultery.
- Thou shalt not covet your neighbor's possessions.
- Honor your mother and father.

This simple code of civil morality has historically insured the morally sane society that almost all nonhumanists desire. It should be the responsibility of government to maintain a climate that is conducive to this kind of moral behavior.

Servants of God   "Why are we here?" The Bible-taught individual finds this an easy question to answer. Our chief purpose is to glorify God by obeying Him and serving our fellowman (*see* Revelation 4:11; Romans 6:11–13, 12:1–2; 1 Corinthians 6:19–20). Nowhere does Scripture instruct us to "Do your own thing." We have a solemn responsibility to serve God, for He made us, died for us, and provided us His wisdom to live by.

Interestingly enough, the happiest, most-fulfilled, and most-contented people in our land are those who obey God. Unlike our autonomous, self-centered humanist friends, believers know who they are, why they are here, and how they should live. By contrast, on college campuses across the land, brilliant young people, studying with learned, experienced teachers, are facing what they call an identity crisis. It should not astonish you that, in spite of limitless li-braries, microfiche, computers, and the finest media presentations, today's collegians are bewildered by the *who* and *why* of human exis-tence. One fundamental law of teaching states, "You cannot impart what you do not possess." Contem-porary humanistic professors, curric-ula molders, and textbook writers do not themselves know the answers to these questions.

No Christian should ever suffer from identity crisis! If you have re-ceived Jesus Christ as your Saviour and Lord, it is clear who you are: You are a child of God and a servant of God. The why has likewise been revealed: Your purpose on earth is to serve Him. This concept largely explains why Christians have always been the great humanitarians of the world. Historically, they have built the orphanages, hospitals, schools, homes for unwed mothers, and so forth. I have never heard of humanists con-structing such humanitarian projects with their own money. Their method is to infiltrate and take over such ministries, get-ting them financed with taxpayers' money, while they infuse their humanist principles. They call this progress. Frankly, if the degenerate path we have traveled in this country during the past three decades of humanist domination is *progress,* we owe Sodom and Gomorrah an apology. As a counselor, I can testify that the increased breakdown of the home, alcoholism, suicide, homosexuality, and drug addiction (which I lay primarily at the door of the humanist educators and their disciples, who are temporarily our government leaders) are hardly indications that the humanist philosophy produces happiness.

Jesus Christ said, "Happy is he that hears the word of God and keeps it" (*see* Luke 11:28). Millions of happily married couples within the moral majority of our nation's population testify that our Saviour's promise is still valid.

Compassionate World View   The world view that the apostle Paul calls the wisdom of God is twofold: temporal and future.

The *temporal* view in the Old Testament challenged the Jews to be God's torchbearers. Since the good news about God is not known innately through man's wisdom, God instructed the Jews to communicate this Old Testament message to the heathen nations.

New Testament Christians have been given the Great Commission, challenging them to ... "Go into all the world and preach the gospel to every creature" (Mark 16:15 NKJB-NT). The Bible looks upon the world of separate nations as a spiritual field of people ripe unto harvest (*see* Matthew 13:1–23). For that reason, almost 60,000 American Christians are serving in foreign countries as missionaries.

The second part of the biblical world view is the *future* promise of eternal life, an age of peace, righteousness, justice, and a new eternal earth that most believers refer to as "heaven" (*see* Isaiah 65 and 66; Revelation 20–22). The various denominations do not agree about the specific nature of the next life, but *all* recognize that one will exist. The entire revelation of God, both Old and New Testaments, repeatedly refers to a future life after death. The Bible is unquestionably a book of resurrection.

Summary

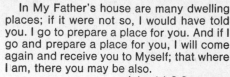

In My Father's house are many dwelling places; if it were not so, I would have told you. I go to prepare a place for you. And if I go and prepare a place for you, I will come again and receive you to Myself; that where I am, there you may be also.

John 14:2,3 NKJB-NT

. . . your body is the temple of the Holy Spirit who is in you . . . and you are not your own. For you were bought at a price; therefore glorify God in your body and in your spirit, which are God's.

1 Corinthians 6:19,20 NKJB-NT

. . . blessed are they that hear the word of God, and keep it.

Luke 11:28

God created man in his own image, in the image of God created he him; male and female created he them.

Genesis 1:27

In the beginning God. . . .

Genesis 1:1

THE WISDOM OF GOD

4

Humanism:
The Wisdom of Man

Humanism is not only the world's greatest evil but, until recently, the most deceptive of all religious philosophies. Early in

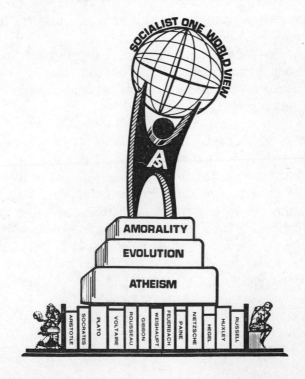

its history, the humanists developed a vocabulary of their own and applied the art of semantics to their indoctrination. That is, they used words describing their concepts that meant one thing to parents with traditional moral values and another thing to students of humanism. So clever has been their purposeful use of this art that millions of nonhumanists have been duped by their designs, naively accepting some of their teachings.

One well-informed history professor, who heard I was writing this book, declared, "It is impossible for the noncollege-trained person to understand humanism." I don't believe that! In fact, both the noncollege- and college-trained individual only need to have the ambiguous terms of humanism simplified, to not only understand it, but to reject it. And that starts with the five basic tenets of humanism pictured on the preceding page.

First, we shall examine them individually, through the statements of leading humanist authorities. In chapter five, we shall inspect them within the official humanist Bible, and in chapter six, we shall demonstrate their unscientific basis.

It is not reason that causes a person to disbelieve in God. Only prejudice—that is, a preconceived judgment—can convert an individual to atheism. If his conclusion were based solely on reason, the evidence so strongly favors belief in God that unbiased people must accept the reality of His existence.

In recent years, humanists have become so powerful that they no longer try to conceal their true interests but openly acknowledge their beliefs. They are convinced that it is too late for the pro-moral people of our country to eject them from offices or positions of public trust and influence. I do not agree! I am convinced that if we expose the teachings and intentions of humanism to enough people, we can yet return moral sanity to our land. It will start with a clear understanding of what a humanist really believes.

The Five Basic Tenets of Humanism

The five basic tenets of humanism, which make up their destructive world view, are adapted from the writings of their own leading authorities.

Atheism The foundation stone of all humanistic thought is atheism: the belief that there is no God. Descartes, the famous French philosopher who tried to project his mind out into the universe, finally concluded with the well-known epithet, "I think, therefore I am." This deification of man launched the

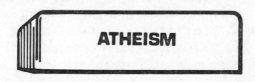

Age of Reason (the worship of man's wisdom). It was picked up by French skeptics, primarily Voltaire and Rousseau, and was then developed by German rationalists like Georg Hegel, Ludwig Feuerbach, and Friedrich Nietzche, until they reached the verdict, "God is dead." The modern existentialist speaks the current humanist thought by urging, "The idea of God is self-contradictory."

Dr. Corliss Lamont, a leading spokesman for humanism for over thirty years, in his definitive book *The Philosophy of Humanism,* makes the following statements that establish its atheistic base:

> First, Humanism believes in a naturalistic metaphysics or attitude toward the universe that considers all forms of the supernatural as myth; and that regards Nature as the totality of being and as a constantly changing system of matter and energy which exists independently of any mind or consciousness.[17]

Humanism believes that Nature itself constitutes the sum

total of reality, that matter-energy and not mind is the foundation stuff of the universe, and that supernatural entities simply do not exist. This nonreality of the supernatural means, on the human level, that men do not possess supernatural and immortal souls; and, on the level of the universe as a whole, that our cosmos does not possess a supernatural and eternal God.[18]

For Humanism the central concern is always the happiness of man in this existence, not in some fanciful never-never land beyond the grave; a happiness worthwhile as an end in itself and not subordinate to or dependent on a Supreme Deity, an invisible King, ruling over the earth and the infinite cosmos.[19]

The originator of the useful word *agnostic* was Thomas H. Huxley, noted English biologist and popularizer of the Darwinian theory. Since agnostics are doubtful about the supernatural, they tend to be Humanists in practice.[20]

Surprisingly enough, atheism is not a very old concept and is rarely mentioned by the ancients. For most of man's history, the existence of God seemed a logical conclusion for anyone who saw His creative handiwork—the firmament, the stars, animals, and man. As education expanded throughout Europe, however, atheism increased; even today, surveys reveal that the higher a person has advanced in education, the more likely he is to be atheistic.

Evolution   Since humanists reject a belief in God, they must next explain man's existence independent of God. For this they resurrect one of the oldest religious beliefs of all time: the theory of evolution, which can be traced back to Babylon 2,000

EVOLUTION

years before Christ (*see The Troubled Waters of Evolution,* by Henry M. Morris).

The theory of evolution, although ancient, was catapulted into world prominence by the publication of Charles Darwin's *The Origin of Species.* "Darwinism," as it came to be known, swept through the atheistic- or agnostic-dominated academic community of the Western world like wildfire. Today it is the primary foundation upon which all secular education rests. Psychology, the most influential single discipline of modern education, is totally dependent on the theory of evolution, as are such fields as sociology, political science, biology, and many others. It has had a drastic influence on art, music, and literature. Some informed educators admit that it is the most powerful influence in education today—even though not one of Darwin's "scientific" theories can be proved 120 years later. Even Thomas Huxley, one of the leading exponents of evolution, had to admit that "evolution was not an established theory but a tentative hypothesis, an extremely valuable and even probable hypothesis, but an hypothesis none the less."[21] Dr. D'Arcy Thompson concedes:

> In the study of evolution and in our attempts to trace the descent of the animal kingdom, our score years' study of *The Origin of Species,* has had an unlooked for and disappointing result. It . . . has not taught us how birds descended from reptiles, mammals from other quadrupeds, quadrupeds from fishes, nor vertebrates from the invertebrate stock. The invertebrates themselves involve the selfsame difficulties, so that we do not know the origin of the echinoderms, of the molluscs, of the coelenterates, nor one group of protozoa from another. . . . This failure to solve the cardinal problems of evolutionary biology is a very curious thing.[22]

Evidence that all scientists do not accept the theory of evolution appears in Duncan's book with the following statement by a well-known biologist of the Smithsonian Institute:

There is no evidence which would show man developing step by step from lower forms of life. There is nothing to show that man was in any way connected with monkeys. . . . He appeared SUDDENLY and in substantially the same form as he is today. . . . There are no such things as missing links. . . . So far as concerns the major groups of animals, the creationists appear to have the best of the argument. There is NOT THE SLIGHTEST EVIDENCE THAT ANY ONE OF THE MAJOR GROUPS AROSE FROM ANY OTHER. Each is a special animal complex, related more or less closely to all the rest, and appearing therefore as a special and distinct creation.[23]

Why do humanists hold so zealously to the theory of evolution and become emotionally upset when Institute for Creation Research scientists confront them with its scientific weakness? Quite simply, their *belief* in man independent of God is dependent on it. The controversy raging over the prospect of teaching creation alongside evolution in the public schools springs from the humanists' fear that if the theory of evolution is discredited, as they are apprehensive it may be, their entire humanist philosophy will collapse.

Humanists are committed evolutionists. Corliss Lamont explains it this way:

. . . biology has conclusively shown that man and all other forms of life were the result, not of a supernatural act of creation by God, but of an infinitely long process of evolution probably stretching over at least two billion years. In that gradual evolutionary advance which started with the lowly amoeba and those even simpler things marking the transition from inanimate matter to life, body was prior and basic. With its increasing complexity, there came about an accompanying development and integration of animal behavior and control, culminating in the species man and in the phenomenon called mind. Mind, in short, appeared at the present apex of the evolutionary process and not at the beginning.[24]

Like all humanists, Lamont believes that man is an animal, for he notes, "Man, like the higher primates from which he is descended, is a gregarious creature. . . ."[25] He boasts, "Biologically speaking, the animal, man, has been an enormous success."[26]

Sir Julian Huxley, one of the founders of the prestigious American Humanist Association, defined humanism in these words:

> I use the word "humanist" to mean someone who believes that man is just as much a natural phenomenon as an animal or plant; that his body, mind and soul were not supernaturally created but are products of evolution, and that he is not under the control or guidance of any supernatural being or beings, but has to rely on himself and his own powers.[27]

Many other statements by humanists could be used to substantiate their obsessive belief in evolution. In the next chapter, I shall quote from the *Humanist Manifesto,* regarded as the official bible of humanism, to verify that this unscientific theory is a major part of official humanist doctrine.

An engineer in our city attended church regularly with his wife, though personally he was an atheist. Finally he invited me to his home, saying, "I have three questions. If you can satisfactorily answer them, I will become a Christian."

Providentially, I had been led to study those three questions just the week before, so for two hours, I presented him with the logical, Bible-based answers he needed. When we finished, I asked, "Does that answer all your questions?"

He replied, "Yes. I didn't realize there were such answers."

Then I asked, "Are you now ready to accept Christ?"

He responded, "Let's not be too hasty. I don't want to rush into anything!"

As far as I know, he is still a skeptic; but his skepticism, like all atheism, is based on neither logic nor fact.

It is impossible to overestimate the influence that evolution has exercised upon our society. Former Congressman John Conlan and attorney John Whitehead recognized this when they stated, "Evolution has altered the course of history by shifting the base of moral absolutes from traditional theism to Secular Humanism."[28]

AMORALITY

Amorality   The humanistic doctrine of evolution has naturally led to the destruction of the moral foundation upon which this country was originally built. If you believe that man is an animal, you will naturally expect him to live like one. Consequently, almost every sexual law that is required in order to maintain a morally sane society has been struck down by the humanists, so that man may follow his animal appetites. Such was predicted in *The Humanist* magazine some years back: ". . . Darwin's discovery of the principle of evolution sounded the death knell of religious and moral values. It removed the ground from under the feet of traditional religion."[29]

It certainly has not been the Bible-believing churches of our nation that have advocated sexual permissiveness; trial marriages; easy divorce; abortion-on-demand; inflammatory sex education forcibly taught our school children from kindergarten through high school; coed college dorms; homosexuality as an optional life-style; and free access to pornography, marijuana, and occasionally, hard drugs. This country's leading humanistic educators, lawmakers, and judges have consistently liberalized our statutes in these areas. They are committed to doing away with every vestige of the responsible, moral behavior that distinguished man from animals.

The humanists' overt hostility toward Christianity is nowhere more apparent than in their successful attempt in the last three decades to destroy almost all biblical moral standards in our country. This is due to their rejection of God and His authority over them, which determines what is right or wrong. As one leading "sexologist" (as they like to call themselves) said, with her finger pointed toward the sky, "There is no one up there telling you what is right and wrong."

In other words, there are no absolutes!

"The only thing that is absolute is that there is nothing absolute!" These are the words a philosophy professor uses to begin his course of study. Such an assault on young, impressionable minds flies in the face of revealed truth: 3,500 years of Judeo-Christian morality, the Reformation, and everything that is good and wholesome in Western culture. No humanists have come forward to prove there are no absolutes. They just keep dogmatically repeating this maxim to one another and to anyone else who will listen, vainly hoping that believing it will make it so.

This philosophy of no absolutes has opened the door to "situation ethics," "permissiveness," "free love," "sexually active youth," and a whole vocabulary of code words for adultery, fornication, perversion, abomination, and just plain *sin*. Junior-high-school through college youth, the target of humanist amoral teachings for the past two decades, have become vulnerable to enormous immorality. One high-school principal recently admitted, "Twenty percent of our senior class has either had, or is a carrier of, a venereal disease." Surveys show that girls graduating from high school as virgins are now in the minority.

Dr. Albert Ellis, along with other humanists, has long been an advocate of situation ethics. In the September–October

1969 issue of *The Humanist,* he is quoted as saying, "What are the main principles of humanistic ethics, from which the principles of sexual ethics can be logically derived? No one seems to know for sure, since variant and absolutistic ethical ideals do not seem to be achievable; nor are they particularly human." When a doctor of philosophy stands before students or sex-education teachers and states that moral or ethical absolutes are not "human," it is only natural that he will discard such precepts as "Thou shalt not commit adultery."

The amoral teachings of the humanists, who provide the sex-education materials, movies, books, magazines, and so forth for the public schools throughout the nation, are not presented in the abstract, but in terms their students can clearly understand. Consider this advice—taken from Claire Chambers's *The SIECUS Circle*—on sexual experimentation by SIECUS president Dr. Mary Calderone, who was declared Humanist of the Year in 1974 by the American Humanist Association:

> *On sexual experimentation:* The adolescent years are, among other things, for learning how to integrate sex usefully and creatively into daily living. Therefore, we must accept that adolescent sexual experimentation is not just inevitable, but actually necessary for normal development.
>
> *On premarital sex:* I advocate discussion of it, so that young people know they have choices beginning with masturbation, of course, and petting to climax and mutual orgasm before moving on to intercourse.
>
> *On extramarital sex:* An extramarital affair that's really solid might have very good results.
>
> *On* Sexology *magazine: Sexology* magazine is no more pornographic than the Bible.

There is no greater evidence of the humanists' obsession with sexual license than the fact that the leaders of the sexual revolution of the 70s were overwhelmingly humanists. The sex-education authors, publishers, and SIECUS board members who proclaim homosexuality as an optional life-style to our school children are humanists.

Many do not realize that most of the leaders of the feminist movement, which presents itself as the preserver of sexual rights of women and children, are humanists. Betty Friedan, for example, won the Humanist of the Year award in 1975. Toni Carabillo, past vice-president of NOW, declared, "I don't think the women's movement, as such, is going to remain a women's movement. I think as more understand what we are really saying, the 10 percent male membership we now have will begin to swell. I think we'll stop describing ourselves as feminists and begin to describe ourselves as humanists and really begin to deal with the problems of creating a different kind of society."[30]

Don't think for a moment that the amoral humanists are satisfied, now that perversion is recognized as normal in some areas of our country. They will not stop until it is universally recognized. They are really after the young, who will be the key to humanist control of the next generation. That is why— in the name of "health care," "child's rights," "child abuse," and "the Year of the Child"—they are pressuring political leaders to pass legislation taking the control of children away from their parents and giving it to the state. By *the state,* of course, they mean bureaucrats and social-change agents who have been carefully trained in amoral, humanistic philosophy and who will use the government's power to teach sexual activity, contraceptives, birth elimination, and permissiveness to children, whether parents want it or not! Of course, government-financed abortions will be provided for those who fail to follow instructions.

What morally minded people perceive as the bizarre and unbelievable actions and policies of educators, social workers, and government bureaucrats are the natural result of their basic beliefs.

Consider Dr. Lamont again: "Morally speaking, the sex life of an individual is no more important than his political or economic life."[31] Morally speaking, we would add, one's actions reflect his beliefs.

Lamont clarifies his ethical position as follows: "For Humanism no human acts are good or bad in or of themselves. Whether an act is good or bad is to be judged by its *consequences* for the individual and society. Knowledge of the good, then, must be worked out, like knowledge of anything else, through the examination and evaluation of the concrete consequences of an idea or hypothesis. Humanist ethics draws its guiding principles from human experience and tests them in human experience."[32] The truly moral person will be obliged to "discard the outmoded ethics of the past. . . . The merely good is the enemy of the better. The Humanist refuses to accept any Ten Commandments or other ethical precepts as immutable and universal laws never to be challenged or questioned. He bows down to no alleged supreme moral authority either past or present."[33] The humanist intensely rejects "the puritanical prejudice against pleasure and desire that marks the Western tradition of morality. Men and women have profound wants and needs of an emotional and physical character, the fulfillment of which is an essential ingredient in the good life. Contempt for or suppression of normal desires may result in their discharge in surreptitious, coarse, or abnormal ways."[34] The author fails to advise that suppression of normal desires may also develop character and self-discipline. Obviously humanism not only conceives of man as an animal, but as an amoral animal.

Autonomous Man   Humanists view man as an autonomous, self-centered, godlike person with unlimited goodness and potential—if his environment is controlled to let his free spirit develop. One of the worst sins of man (according to humanists) is not the killing of innocent, unborn children through abortion, or even the murder of preemies or children born with defects; it is inhibiting the liberty and freedom of another to express himself.

That man is innately good and capable of solving the problems of man independent of any Supreme Being is a consistent assumption of humanism's philosophy that "Man is the measure of all things." This concept, first coined by Protagoras, a Greek philosopher of the fifth century B.C., has since become a basic tenet of humanism. Jean Jacques Rousseau (1712–1778), the French skeptic, is probably a most influential writer-philosopher for today's college youth. They study him vigorously, and most humanistic college professors are well versed in his thinking. Rousseau said, "If man is good by nature, as I believe to have shown him to be, it follows that he stays like that as long as nothing foreign to him corrupts him."

Incidentally, professors who eulogize this hero of the Enlightenment rarely tell their students that, in his personal life, Rousseau was a moral degenerate. For sixteen years he lived outside the bounds of marriage with his mistress in Paris, who bore him five illegitimate sons—all of whom he abandoned in the Paris General Hospital. Humanist theorists may exalt that kind of autonomous, self-centered thinking as "self-actualization" at its best, but I can't help wishing that someone had preserved testimony from the victims of his self-ishness—his five orphaned sons.

Nearly three centuries later, the modern humanist Lamont adds to Rousseau's dictum:

> What the scientific study of human motives shows is that human nature is neither essentially bad nor essentially good, neither essentially selfish nor essentially unselfish, neither essentially warlike nor essentially pacific. There is neither original sin nor original virtue. But human nature is essentially flexible and educable. And the moulding or re-moulding of human motives is something that takes place not only in childhood and youth, but also throughout adult life and under the impact of fundamental economic institutions and cultural media that weightily influence mind and character. The social development and conditioning of human beings, their training, direct and indirect, by means of all sorts of educational techniques, can be so extensive that the hoary half-truth, "You can't change human nature," becomes quite irrelevant.[35]

Dr. Schaeffer points out that autonomous thinking historically leads not to world betterment, or even human improvement, but to chaos. Rousseau's philosophy, for example, was a major factor in producing the French Revolution, which was not only chaos for the royalty but also for the poor people. Man is not autonomous, but dependent on God. He finds his greatest fulfillment when he is aware of that fact.

Self-centered, self-sufficient man. Once man thinks he is independent of God, he becomes self-centered; suddenly he and his wants become the measure of all things. Today's philosophy of education is obsessed with self-actualization, self-sufficiency, self-satisfaction. Consider the following:

> Humanism is the viewpoint that men have but one life to lead and should make the most of it in terms of creative work and happiness; that human happiness is its own justification

and requires no sanction or support from supernatural sources; that in any case the supernatural, usually conceived of in the form of heavenly gods or immortal heavens, does not exist; and that human beings, using their own intelligence and co-operating liberally with one another, can build an enduring citadel of peace and beauty upon this earth.[36]

The watchword of Humanism is happiness for all humanity in this existence as contrasted with salvation for the individual soul in a future existence and the glorification of a supernatural Supreme Being. Humanism urges men to accept freely and joyously the great boon of life and to realize that life in its own right and for its own sake can be as beautiful and splendid as any dream of immortality.[37]

. . . Humanism asserts that man's own reason and efforts are man's best and, indeed, only hope; and that man's refusal to recognize this point is one of the chief causes of his failures throughout history. The Christian West has been confused and corrupted for almost 2,000 years by the idea so succinctly expressed by St. Augustine, "Cursed is everyone who places his hope in man."[38]

Starting from an atheistic base, autonomous humanists emphasize *feeling* rather than responsibility. The idea that "If it feels good, it must be good" permeates the land. Did you ever try to reason with a marijuana user or drug addict or an alcoholic? Feelings predominate, for the self-centered human. The fact that he is destroying himself and his culture doesn't dissuade the humanist from doing his own thing. Dr. Schaeffer points out, "As the Christian consensus dies, there are not many sociological alternatives. One possibility is hedonism, in which every man does his own thing. Trying to build a society on hedonism leads to chaos."[39]

We have more selfish people living in our country today than at any other time in history—and do you know why? There are two basic reasons: the self-centered philosophy of humanism and the humanistic ideas of psychology, which have taught permissiveness in child raising, instead of parental discipline. Children raised without loving parental correction grow up to be self-centered and selfish individuals, whose attempt to be independent, or autonomous, leads them to futility, or chaos.

A TV talk-show host once asked me, "On the basis of your counseling experience, what is the primary cause of marital disharmony today?"

My response was immediate: "Selfishness!" In actuality, the root cause of *all* social disharmony is selfishness. An indulgent attitude toward self begets the childish "I want my way" syndrome, causing an individual to stalk through life in an undisciplined, insensitive, unbridled fashion. He will seek to get, rather than give; lust, rather than love; demand, rather than contribute. What happens when his peers act the same way? They incur dissension, hostility, even open combat.

Man is a dependent creature; dependent first on God, then on his fellowman. His failure to recognize that need cheats him, both in this life and the eternity to come.

Socialist One-World View Humanists have a running romance with big government. They universally assume that government is good and that big government is better than little government. Their practical interpretation of *democracy* seems to be freedom only for the individual living within a socialist government, controlled of course, by humanists. The historical facts of life have somehow escaped their attention. That is, they overlook or reject the premise that freedom has always been in inverse proportion to the size and power of government. The less

government, the more freedom—and vice versa.

Anyone familiar with humanist writers is struck by their consistent hostility toward Americanism, capitalism, and free enterprise. But at the same time, they extol the virtues and benefits of socialism, without acknowledging its historical failures. Lamont, one of the chief propagandists for humanism during the last fifty years, repeatedly calls for "a general disarmament" or "collective security." He eulogizes a government that does away with "poverty, unemployment, inflation, depression, business monopoly," for "until we do so there will be no lasting international peace."[40]

What he fails to point out is that this requires virtual economic control by government—in other words, socialism. To reach their goal of a socialist world order by the year 2,000, they do not have time to socialize the world gradually. It must be done quickly, by force and violence, and that is Communism. But that doesn't bother humanists. They are much more respectful of Communism than they are of free enterprise, anyway. Consider these glowing tributes to Marxism:

> The Dialectical Materialism of Marx and Engels corrected the mechanistic errors of the earlier materialist tradition and gave full recognition to the dynamic, ever-changing character of existence and to the infinite interrelatedness of a phenomena in both Nature and society. While Dialectical Materialism considers that human thought is a function of the bodily organism, it believes that the mind is no mere passive reflector of the outside world, but that it possesses a fundamental initiative and creativity, a power of working upon and remolding the environment through the force of new ideas.
>
> At the same time the Marxist materialists have carried on and developed the intransigent antireligious doctrines of the materialists who preceded them. Today there can be little question that Dialectical Materialism, while having its own shortcomings, is the most influential variety of Materialism,

both because of its consistency and inclusiveness and also because it is the official philosophy of Communist governments and parties throughout the world.[41]

The humanists discovered early that the UN offered them a tremendous springboard to a humanist one-world government with a socialistic economic system. In 1966, the *Humanist* magazine for July/August admitted humanism's purpose was to supersede nationalistic boundaries by a worldwide organization that would possess international sovereignty over the nations of the world. Naturally, they believe the UN provides them such a vehicle, which is why so many American leaders in the many UN organizations are committed humanists. For example, three leading members of the American Humanism Association have been directors-general of three prestigious UN organizations: Julian Huxley for UNESCO, Brock Chisholm, who directed the World Health Organization, and Lord Boyd Orr, who was the head of the UN Food and Agriculture Organization.

Claire Chambers clarifies the point further in *The SIECUS Circle*:

> It is no coincidence that Humanists have been planted in a number of strategic positions of influence at the U.N. in recent years to carry out the goals of Huxley, Chisholm, Orr, and others. Although any number of U.N. agencies might be selected at random as illustrations of this, such an undertaking would require a chapter to itself. UNESCO has been singled out as a case in point.
>
> Shortly after UNESCO'S founding, Humanist Ashley Montagu headed the committee that drafted UNESCO's 1950 Statement on Race. Further, various UNESCO publications are generously seasoned with Humanist rhetoric. Two prime examples are UNESCO's quarterly journal, *Impact of Science on Society,* founded in 1952 by American Humanist Association official Dr. Gerald Wendt, who was then in charge of

world-wide development of science education for UNESCO in Paris; and *International Directory of Philosophy and Philosophers,* coedited by Paul Kurtz, editor of *The Humanist.* Other UNESCO-Humanist entanglements are evident. Frederick H. Burkhardt, formerly a member of *The Humanist's* editorial advisory board, has served as chairman of the U.S. National Commission for UNESCO. But more significant is the fact that Humanist Gerald Wendt was for many years president of the UNESCO Publications Center in New York City. Although Wendt is now dead, his widow continues to work in the capacity of secretary for the Publications Center.[42]

As Lamont says, "A truly Humanist civilization must be a world civilization."[43] If humanists can control UNESCO, UNICEF, the UN's World Health Organization, and its food and agriculture organization, they are a long way toward implementing that world civilization. If you think they haven't been very effective, you are kidding yourself. I have a five-volume set of reports entitled *Towards World Understanding* (a 1950 UNESCO publication), that outlines the humanization and socialization of American education. Public education today is exactly as they planned it. In a future book, I will expose that in detail.

So enthusiastic have humanists become in their zeal for a one-world order that, according to Chambers:

... in 1971, some of their leaders combined forces with leading advocates of population control and nationalized abortion, World Federalists, and others, in the formation of the American Movement for World Government. This group's full-page advertisement in the *New York Times* of July 27, 1971, called for a "world federal government to be open at all times to all nations without right of secession," with the power to curb overpopulation.

Other essentials supported by this group of twenty-six signatories of the *Times* ad are a "civilian executive branch with the power to enforce world laws directly upon individuals" (which would automatically supersede the U.S. Constitution); and the "control of all weapons of mass destruction by the world government with the disarmament of all nations, under careful inspection, down to the level required for internal policing." (The latter, of course, could conceivably allow for the stationing of Russian or Chinese Communist troops on U.S. soil.) And, as was further stated in the ad, ". . . a federal world government must be established at the earliest possible moment by basic transformation of the UN or other reasonable means."[44]

This document was not signed by a few socialistic crazies but by the *Who's Who* of humanism.

And that brings us to the important subject of patriotism, or old-fashioned love for one's country. All committed humanists are one-worlders first and Americans second. Hear Corliss Lamont, the doctrinaire humanist:

> All individuals of all countries are together fellow citizens of our one world and fellow members of our one human family. The Americans, the Russians, the English, the Indians, the Chinese, the Germans, the Africans, and the rest are all part of the same perplexed, proud, and aspiring human race.
>
> Humanism is not only a philosophy with a world ideal, but is an ideal philosophy for the world. It is quite conceivable that a majority of this planet's population could come to see the truth of its underlying principles. The Humanist viewpoint, surmounting all national and sectional provincialisms, provides a concrete opportunity for overcoming the age-long cleavage between East and West. Even those who cling to some form of supernaturalism can unite with Humanists, as they did during World War II, on a program of democracy and progress that reaches to the farthest corners of the earth. Humanism is a supranational, panhuman philosophy of universal relevance; it is the philosophic counterpart of world patriotism.[45]

It rejects the dead ends of despair as well as the daydreams of Utopia. I believe firmly that man, who has shown himself to be a very tough animal, has the best part of his career still before him. And there is at least the possibility that by the close of this century "the Humanist breakthrough," in Sir Julian Huxley's phrase, will spread throughout the globe to create a higher civilization of world dimensions.[46]

If that isn't clear enough, consider another statement by Lamont:

Certain forms of modern nationalism—fanatical, intolerant, militaristic, and contemptuous of foreign peoples—amount in essence to the large-scale organization of egoism. They clearly clash with the ideals of Humanism and put current meaning into Dr. Samuel Johnson's remark that "Patriotism is the last refuge of a scoundrel." To love one's country does not really imply that one must hate other countries or adopt the slogan "My country right or wrong." The principle around which the United Nations and the International Court of Justice are organized is that the scope of national sovereignty must be curtailed and that nations must be willing to accept, as against what they conceive to be their own self-interest the democratically arrived at decisions of the world community.[47]

Do you believe that "Patriotism is the last refuge of a scoundrel"? Do your elected political leaders? If they are humanists, they do. And that is one of the chief reasons our politicians have turned the most powerful country in the world after World War II into a neutralized state; they are more interested in world socialism than in America.

That is why humanist politicians permitted Russia to conquer the satellite countries of Europe and turn them into socialist prisons. That is why we were not permitted to win in Korea and Vietnam and why they voted to give away the Panama Canal. That is why Russia was allowed to turn Cuba into an armed camp with a submarine base, stationing at least 3,000 Russian troops, and who knows what else, there?

No humanist is qualified to hold any governmental office in America—United States senator, congressman, cabinet member, State Department employee, or any other position that requires him to think in the best interest of America. He is a socialist one-worlder first, an American second.

The giveaway of the Panama Canal is a prime example of whose team is number one in the hearts of American humanist politicians. America lost on that deal, but socialist and Communist countries all gained. Fortunately, that action was so flagrant that many of the legislators who voted away the canal we purchased and built are being replaced at each election. I am not saying that anyone who voted for the giveaway to the Communist government of Panama is an evil person. I am asserting that the issue stands as an example of the humanist philosophy functioning in the political sphere: Their first allegiance is to a socialist one-world view, then to America. Such politicians can be counted on to vote the same way on other issues: the continuing persecution of Rhodesia; permitting Cuban troops to enslave various African countries such as Angola; breaking off relations with Taiwan; or increasing United States appropriations to the UN.

A humanist is just not qualified to be elected to public office by patriotic, America-loving citizens. The major problems of our day—moral, educational, economical, and governmental—are primarily caused by the fact that over 50 percent of our legislators are either committed humanists or are severely influenced in their thinking by the false theories of humanism.

Humanism's Hostility to Christianity

The spirit of tolerance that is so often extolled in humanist teachings does not extend to Christianity. Knowledgeable humanists look upon the church and its doctrinal absolutes as the greatest enemy of mankind. More than an enemy, the church is a threat to humanism, for its leaders recognize that the only group that can save the Western world from the humanistic mind control of the Communist countries is the church. If Christ's church becomes sufficiently aroused to the fact that humanism is currently winning the battle for the mind, she will awaken the other millions of pro-moral Americans, and together they will vote their amoral humanist overlords out of office and replace them with traditional, pro-moral leaders.

Consider these comments from Lamont and other humanists:

> Passing to the New Testament, we see plainly that its theology, taken literally, is totally alien to the Humanist viewpoint.[48]

> In academic circles Andrew D. White's scholarly study, *A History of the Warfare of Science with Theology in Christendom,* proved of signal service to the documentation of Humanism by showing that the theologians had fought practically every forward step in scientific investigation since the founding of Christianity, much to the detriment of religion as well as of science.[49]

> Thinkers who claim that complete selfishness is an inborn quality of human beings are taking over and expressing in different languages one of the great errors of Christian ethics, namely, that man is inherently sinful and depraved.[50]

Christianity and humanism are particularly 180 degrees in opposition to each other with regard to the promise of life after death. Having just finished a book on that subject, detailing the carefully revealed events of the future life described in Scripture, I can appreciate the humanist's frustration. Bible-taught Christians approach death with peace and confidence, whereas humanists tend to consider that ultimate meeting with God with fear and trepidation. Humanism is a tragic philosophy to live by and a disastrous philosophy to die by. Consider Lamont and William James on immortality:

HUMANISM   CHRISTIANITY

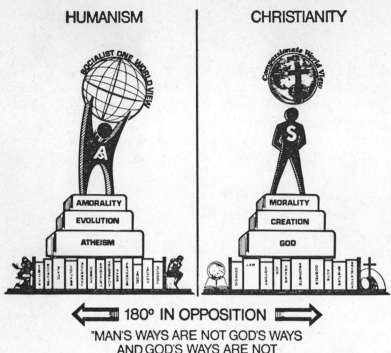

180° IN OPPOSITION

"MAN'S WAYS ARE NOT GOD'S WAYS
AND GOD'S WAYS ARE NOT
MAN'S WAY"   ISAIAH 55:8

The issue of mortality versus immortality is crucial in the argument of Humanism against supernaturalism. For if men realize that their careers are limited to this world, that this earthly existence is all that they will ever have, then they are already more than half-way on the path toward becoming functioning Humanists, no matter what their general attitude toward the universe and no matter what they think about a Deity. In my opinion, the history of philosophy and religion demonstrates that in the West, at least, the idea of immortality has on the whole played a more important part than the idea of God. William James asserts unqualifiedly that "the popular touchstone for all philosophies is the question, 'What is their bearing on a future life?' " If this is true, then James is also correct in observing that for most men God has been primarily the guarantor of survival beyond the grave.

Christianity in particular, with its central emphasis on the resurrection and eternal life, came into being first and foremost as a death-conquering religion.[51]

Consider once again rejection of Christianity and its naive replacement:

Humanism is the viewpoint that. . . . human happiness is its own justification and requires no sanction or support from supernatural sources; that in any case the supernatural, usually conceived of in the form of heavenly gods or immortal heavens, does not exist; and that human beings, using their own intelligence and cooperating liberally with one another, can build an enduring citadel of peace and beauty upon this earth.[52]

One of the greatest complaints of humanism against Christianity is the supposed "censoring" of artistic creativity.

Narrowly moralistic restraints on artists and writers have ever been a bane in the history of the West; and those restraints have frequently stemmed from the supernaturalist's suspicion of earthly pleasures. As Professor Irwin Edman explains: "The traditional quarrel between the artist and the puritan has been the quarrel between those who were frankly interested in the sensuous appearances and surfaces of things and those to whom any involvement or excitement of the senses was a corruption of the spirit or a deflection of some ordered harmony of reason. The history of censorship in the fine arts, if it could be told in full, would be found to revolve in no small measure around the assumed peril of corruption of the spirit by the incitements of the flesh through beautiful things."[53]

Simply interpreted, the artist, *because* he is an artist, must be free to draw his own thing, whether it be an impressionistic blob or a pornographic appeal to the sensual nature. God says, "Thou shalt not. . . ." Humanism says, "Thou shalt!"

The humanist's faith in man and his inherent goodness stands in marked contrast to the Christian position of the Fall. As Lamont admits, "Humanism assigns to man nothing less than the task of being his own saviour."[54] As any Christian knows, man can never save himself. He lost Paradise of his own volition, but he lacks the power and authority to reclaim it. Yet another humanist, John Galsworthy, would dare to claim, "Humanism is the creed of those who believe that in the circle of enwrapping mystery, man's fates are in their own hands—a faith that for modern man is becoming the only possible faith."[55]

If the faith in humanism reflected by the preceding statements has disturbed you, consider the following theory advanced by Lamont, who, you will remember, is an evolutionist. "For a scientifically induced mutation in man may well bring into existence a more advanced species, call it *Superman* or what you will, that will be as superior to us in brain power as we are to the anthropoid ape. Such an outcome is certainly within the realm of biological possibility."[56]

It is frightening to consider what B. F. Skinner and humanist geneticists could do, now that test-tube babies are possible—if the government would permit it. Orwell's *1984* is rapidly approaching! All it takes is for Big Brother to become all-powerful. No wonder Senator Barry Goldwater has warned Americans that we cannot survive another ten years of liberal, humanistic leadership. He really thinks it may be only five.

If that sounds pessimistic, it is only because we have been concentrating on the problems. There are abundant resources available to us, and they will be presented in a later chapter.

HUMANISM: THE WISDOM OF MAN

Summary

Humanism is pro-one world—America second, with an obsession to merge Western democracies, Eastern Communism, and third-world dictatorships into a one-world, socialist state, where Plato's dream of "three classes of people" would be fulfilled:

- The elite *ruling class*
- The omnipresent *military*
- The *masses,* where there is no difference between sexes: Men and women do the same work, and children are wards of the state. Naturally, the humanists will be the elite *ruling class.*

Humanism's premise: Man is basically *good.* His goals should be self-actualization, self-determination, and self-indulgence. Since there is no life after death, it is in man's best interest to find the "good life" here and now. "Do your own thing"; stress human rights; be lenient to criminals.

Humanists advocate sexual activity and promiscuity for the young, as well as the old. They advocate free use of pornography and drugs and endorse prostitution, homosexuality, and abortion-on-demand in the name of human rights. Their guiding principle is "Do what is in your own self-interest," and they are very hostile to Christianity and morality.

Humanists hold a religious theory that permits them to explain man's origin without God—thus leaving man unaccountable to God. In spite of scientific evidence to the contrary, they insist that man is the highest form of primate. They will not permit creation to be given equal time in our so-called "free public schools."

Humanists foster the unscientific religious belief that there is not now and never has been either a Supreme Being or a personal God who is interested in the affairs of man.

5

The Humanist Bible
The Humanist Manifestos
I and II

What the Bible is to Christians, the *Humanist Manifesto* is to humanists. It represents the official position of the humanist movement and is accepted by the faithful as the current mandate on humanist beliefs, values, and goals. Its very existence, which so clearly sets forth their atheistic, evolutionary, amoral, self-worshiping, and socialistic world views, shows how confident humanists are in their ultimate triumph. This amazing document blueprints their takeover of the twenty-first century.

Humanist Manifesto I was compiled by thirty-four liberal humanists in the United States.[57] Many of its signers, like John Dewey, were leaders in the field of education, government, and the Unitarian clergy. *Humanist Manifesto II,* the 1973 update of the previous document, supersedes it, proclaiming itself a "positive declaration for times of uncertainty."[58] The following statements from the manifestos affirm their belief in the five basic tenets of humanism.

Atheism

Religious humanists regard the universe as self-existing and not created. . . .[59] We find insufficient evidence for belief in the existence of a supernatural; it is either meaningless or irrelevant to the question of the survival and fulfillment of the human race. As nontheists, we begin with humans not God,

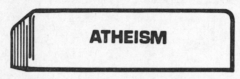

nature not deity. Nature may indeed be broader and deeper than we now know; any new discoveries, however, will but enlarge our knowledge of the natural. . . .[60] But we can discover no divine purpose or providence for the human species. While there is much that we do not know, humans are responsible for what we are or will become. No deity will save us; we must save ourselves.[61]

Evolution

Humanism believes that man is part of nature and that he has emerged as the result of a continuous process. . . .[62] Hold-

ing an organic view of life, humanists find that the traditional dualism of mind and body must be rejected. . . .[63] Humanism recognizes that man's religious culture and civilization, as clearly depicted by anthropology and history, are the product of a gradual development due to his interaction with his natural environment and with his social heritage. The individual born into a particular culture is largely molded to that culture.[64] ... science affirms that the human species is an emergence from natural evolutionary forces. As far as we know, the total personality is a function of the biological organism transacting in a social and cultural context. There is no credible evidence that life survives the death of the body. We continue to exist in our progeny and in the way that our lives have influenced others in our culture.[65]

Amorality

We affirm that moral values derive their source from human experience. Ethics is autonomous and situational, needing no theological or ideological sanction. Ethics stems from human need and interest. To deny this distorts the whole basis of life.[66] In the area of sexuality, we believe that intolerant attitudes, often cultivated by orthodox religions and puritanical

AMORALITY

cultures, unduly repress sexual conduct. The right to birth control, abortion, and divorce should be recognized. While we do not approve of exploitive, denigrating forms of sexual expression, neither do we wish to prohibit, by law or social sanction, sexual behavior between consenting adults. The many varieties of sexual exploration should not in themselves be considered "evil." Without countenancing mindless permissiveness or unbridled promiscuity, a civilized society should be a tolerant one. Short of harming others or compelling them to do likewise, individuals should be permitted to express their sexual proclivities and pursue their life-styles as they desire.

We wish to cultivate the development of a responsible attitude toward sexuality, in which humans are not exploited as sexual objects, and in which intimacy, sensitivity, respect, and honesty in interpersonal relations are encouraged. Moral education for children and adults is an important way of developing awareness and sexual maturity.[67]

It is obvious that this amoral life view is the officially endorsed position of our government and the educational system. For over seventy-five years, judges, legislators, governors, mayors, and presidents have introduced legislation based on this philosophy which is destructive of morality and family solidarity. We have arrived at the gates of Sodom and Gomorrah.

Autonomous, Self-Centered Man

Human life has meaning because we create and develop our futures. Happiness and the creative realization of human needs and desires, individually and in shared enjoyment, are continuous themes of humanism. We strive for the good life, here and now. The goal is to pursue life's enrichment despite debasing forces of vulgarization, commercialization, bureaucratization, and dehumanization. . . .[68] Reason and intelligence are the most effective instruments that humankind possesses. There is no substitute: neither faith nor passion suffices in itself. The controlled use of scientific methods, which have transformed the natural and social sciences since the Renaissance, must be extended further in the solution of human problems. . . .[69] To enhance freedom and dignity the individual must experience a full range of

civil liberties in all societies. This includes freedom of speech and the press, political democracy, the legal right of opposition to governmental policies, fair judicial process, religious liberty, freedom of association, and artistic, scientific, and cultural freedom. It also includes a recognition of an individual's right to die with dignity, euthanasia, and the right to suicide. We oppose the increasing invasion of privacy, by whatever means, in both totalitarian and democratic societies. We would safeguard, extend, and implement the principles of human freedom evolved from the *Magna Carta* to the *Bill of Rights,* the *Rights of Man,* and the *Universal Declaration of Human Rights....*[70] The preciousness and dignity of the individual person is a central humanist value. Individuals should be encouraged to realize their own creative talents and desires. We reject all religious, ideological, or moral codes that denigrate the individual, suppress freedom, dull intellect, dehumanize personality. We believe in maximum individual autonomy consonant with social responsibility. Although science can account for the causes of behavior, the possibilities of individual freedom of choice exist in human life and should be increased.[71]

The purpose of life for the humanist constrasts sharply with that of the Christian. "Religious humanism considers the complete realization of human personality to be the end of man's life and seeks its development and fulfillment in the here and now. This is the explanation of the humanist's social passion."[72] The writers fail to point out that in order to grant such unbridled freedom to everyone, we must remove all restraints. In so doing, we open the door to anarchy. As we have seen, total liberty—or, as they call it, "democracy"—leads to anarchy. Americans have always preferred a government of laws, where the good of the many is preferred to the good of the individual. Otherwise chaos will open the door to a totalitarian dictator. "Democracy" is a fantasy! Men must be governed by moral laws that curb their natural (fleshly) instincts and impose ethical mandates upon their activities. Without such laws,

factions struggle for supremacy, society sinks into a revolutionary state, and dictatorship devours the result.

Socialistic One-World View

Although the humanist prizes individual freedom and
loathes external restraints, for some reason, he yearns for an
international oneness of all people and seems willing to sacrifice national benefits to international unity. While we may
sympathize with his endeavors to help starving masses or improve other cultures, we stand in disbelief at his naive willing-
ness to discard the freedoms guaranteed by American legal
documents (particularly the Bill
of Rights) and place himself
under the rule of international
laws and judicial processes.
Even in our own country, when
we let Big Brother do it, we
complain about red tape, lack of
personal concern, higher prices,
and overall bungling. Can't they
envision the same ineptitude on
an international scale? Regardless of potential disaster, hear
their glowing resolution, as found in the Humanist bible:

> We deplore the division of humankind on nationalistic
> grounds. We have reached a turning point in human history
> where the best option is to transcend the limits of national
> sovereignty and to move toward the building of a world com-
> munity in which all sectors of the human family can partici-
> pate. Thus we look to the development of a system of world
> law and a world order based upon transnational federal gov-
> ernment. This would appreciate cultural pluralism and diver-
> sity. It would not exclude pride in national origins and ac-
> complishments nor the handling of regional problems on a
> regional basis. Human progress, however, can no longer be

achieved by focusing on one section of the world, Western or Eastern, developed or underdeveloped. For the first time in human history, no part of humankind can be isolated from any other. Each person's future is in some way linked to all. We thus reaffirm a commitment to the building of world community, at the same time recognizing that this commits us to some hard choices. . . .[73] The problems of economic growth and development can no longer be resolved by one nation alone; they are worldwide in scope. It is the moral obligation of the developed nations to provide—through an international authority that safeguards human rights—massive technical, agricultural, medical, and economic assistance, including birth control techniques, to the developing portions of the globe. World poverty must cease. Hence extreme disproportions in wealth, income, and economic growth should be reduced on a worldwide basis.[74]

All Christians deplore world poverty. But even if it could be eliminated by world socialism (which it cannot, because socialism stultifies production. For example, socialistic Russia is still dependent on the free world for food), if it came at the expense of control by atheistic, amoral humanists, the price would be too great! Since their philosophy is only unproven theory, which contradicts historical precedent, it is obviously too dangerous a course to follow.

"One worldism" is substantially bolstered by the humanist's egalitarian pose:

The principle of moral equality must be furthered through elimination of all discrimination based upon race, religion, sex, age, or national origin. This means equality of opportunity and recognition of talent and merit. Individuals should be encouraged to contribute to their own betterment. If unable, then society should provide means to satisfy their basic economic, health, and cultural needs, including, wherever resources make possible, a minimum guaranteed annual income.[75]

No other system has been devised that would have a more stultifying impact on creativity and human initiative. What a far cry from "Necessity is the mother of invention." Continuously guaranteed welfarism is the worst human demotivator ever conceived by government.

The humanist's intellectual ideal of peace impels him to declare:

> This world community must renounce the resort to violence and force as a method of solving international disputes. We believe in the peaceful adjudication of differences by international courts and by the development of the arts of negotiation and compromise. War is obsolete. So is the use of nuclear, biological, and chemical weapons. It is a planetary imperative to reduce the level of military expenditures and turn these savings to peaceful and people-oriented uses.[76]

The problem with this idealism is that humanists have a basic misunderstanding of the nature of man. They consider man inherently good, whereas the Bible pictures humanity as fallen, sinful, and untrustworthy. Humanists naively envision a utopian world millennium, when all countries renounce war and man is engulfed by peace, prosperity, and brotherhood. If they would learn a lesson from history, they would find that such a utopian life-style has never existed and never will. Mankind must experience a change in nature before people can live together as brothers in a world of peace. The twenty-seven dictators in Africa prove once again that ruthless man will trample the rights of the weak, if given the chance. In fact, humanist theories have made dictatorships out of these African states.

Humanistic myopia cannot get one principle in focus: a one-world, socialist government must select a supreme governor to make the final decisions, and such a person must be human. History shows that such leaders invariably turn out to

be Stalins, Hitlers, and Maos—rigid, ruthless, ironfisted, dicta-
torial. They have accounted for the deaths of over 65 million of
their own countrymen. Who could possibly imagine that an
international ruler would be humane in his treatment of people
over whom he rules? Only an idealistic humanist!

It is this socialistic, one-world bent of the humanist's mind
that renders him unqualified to hold any government office in
our land—particularly national government. As we shall see,
however, many of our senators, congressmen, cabinet members, and particularly State Department employees during the
past forty years have been humanists. That is why America has
faded from its position as the most powerful nation on earth to
our present status of military inferiority to Russia.

Interestingly enough, the socialist viewpoint does not represent that of the American people, but only that of 600 or so
humanists in the above-mentioned categories, who have
molded the foreign policy of our country since the 1940s. Our
forefathers rebelled at taxation without representation. It is
time that 175 million or more pro-Americans in this country go
to the polls and vote out of office the 600 humanists whose socialistic viewpoints misrepresent them.

The Anti-Biblical Hostility of Humanism

Like the other statements of humanists, the *Humanist Manifesto* is quite clear in its denunciation of traditional religious
beliefs:

> The time has come for widespread recognition of the radical
> changes in religious beliefs throughout the modern world. The
> time is past for mere revision of traditional attitudes. Science
> and economic change have disrupted the old beliefs. Religions
> the world over are under the necessity of coming to terms with
> new conditions created by a vastly increased knowledge and
> experience.[77]

We believe, however, that traditional dogmatic or authoritarian religions that place revelation, God, ritual, or creed above human needs and experience do a disservice to the human species.[78]

As in 1933, humanists still believe that traditional theism, especially faith in the prayer-hearing God, assumed to love and care for persons, to hear and understand their prayers, and to be able to do something about them, is an unproved and outmoded faith. Salvationism, based on mere affirmation, still appears as harmful, diverting people with false hopes of heaven hereafter. Reasonable minds look to other means for survival.[79]

Promises of immortal salvation or fear of eternal damnation are both illusory and harmful. They distract humans from present concerns, from self-actualization, and from rectifying social injustices. Modern science discredits such historic concepts as the "ghost in the machine" and the "separable soul."[80]

Today man's larger understanding of the universe, his scientific achievements, and his deeper appreciation of brotherhood, have created a situation which requires a new statement of the means and purposes of religion. Such a vital, fearless, and frank religion capable of furnishing adequate social goals and personal satisfactions may appear to many people as a complete break with the past. While this age does own a vast debt to traditional religions, it is none the less obvious that any religion that can hope to be a synthesizing and dynamic force for today must be shaped for the needs of this age. To establish such a religion is a major necessity of the present.[81]

Humanism's Goals

The next century can be and should be the humanistic century. Dramatic scientific, technological, and ever-accelerating social and political changes crowd our awareness. We have virtually conquered the planet, explored the moon, overcome the natural limits of travel and communication; we stand at the dawn of a new age, ready to move farther into space and perhaps inhabit other planets.[82]

Religious humanism maintains that all associations and institutions exist for the fulfillment of human life. The intelligent evaluation, transformation, control, and direction of such associations and institutions with a view to the enhancement of human life is the purpose and program of humanism. Certainly religious institutions, their ritualistic forms, ecclesiastical methods, and communal activities must be reconstituted as rapidly as experience allows in order to function effectively in the modern world.[83]

Do you see what they are really saying?

The humanists want to control the lives and destinies of the world's peoples, and they intend their takeover by the twenty-first century. What they fail to realize is that if they so disarm and destroy the United States that we become vulnerable to a Communist overthrow, they would be among the first people the Communists would eliminate. Humanist ideals are permissible in a republic that guarantees freedom of expression, but they are even now unacceptable thought forms in totalitarian Russia, China, or Cuba. If you don't believe that, ask the 12 million political prisoners in the Gulag Archipelago.

The tenets of humanism described in the two *Humanist Manifestos* are not the weird ideas of a few obscure imbeciles unworthy of our consideration. They are the religious beliefs of some of the most influential people in America. Educators lead the list, many of whom are heads of universities or college departments that mold the thinking of those who become the teachers of our school children. Over 160 leading humanists signed the original *Humanist Manifesto II*. Still others were added through the years, until now there are well over 200 who officially recognize its goals.

Since its signing in 1973, humanists have consistently taught its dogma to our youth and used their influence to implement its objectives and lofty ideals.

Summary of
Humanist Manifesto I & II

(read from bottom up)

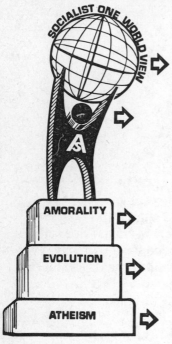

"We have reached a turning point in human history where the best often is to transcend the limits of national sovereignty and move toward the building of a world community . . . the peaceful adjudication of differences by international courts."

"We believe in maximum individual autonomy—reject all religious, moral codes that supress freedom, . . . demand civil liberties, including right to oppose governmental policies—right to die with dignity, euthanasia and suicide."

"Ethics is autonomous and situational . . . and stem from self interest—favor right to birth control, abortion, divorce and choice of sex direction."

"Religious Humanists regard the universe as self-existing and not created. . . . the human species is an emergence from natural evolutionary forces."

"We find insufficient evidence for belief in the existence of the supernatural . . . as nontheists we begin with man not God . . . no deity will save us; we must save ourselves."

6

Humanism Is Unscientific

Humanism is known by a variety of titles today: secular humanism; rationalistic humanism; religious humanism; enlightened humanism. But the favorite term used by the humanists themselves for their religious faith is *scientific humanism.* It appears repeatedly in all their journals, books, and advertisements. Ironically, humanism is completely unscientific! As we shall see in this chapter, not one premise of humanism will stand up to scientific investigation. It is all a zealously defended fraud.

You may well wonder why many educators and people of prominence (educated by educators) freely acknowledge themselves as scientific humanists, when it is really so unscientific. The answer is that they have been brainwashed by the philosophy of humanist John Dewey, the father of progressive (humanistic) education, and his followers. If children are taught to read the words *scientific humanism* as soon as they are old enough to read and humanism is consistently labeled "scientific," they will believe it. In fact, long before the 50 million children in our American school system are old enough to understand humanism or begin to examine it for themselves, they are convinced that it is scientific. After all, their schoolteachers told them it was!

Honest educators within our present humanistically controlled school system must answer one question: Is teaching young people that which is unscientific, as if it were scientific, education or brainwashing? Until the many objective educators still in the public system awaken to the fraud they are perpetrating in the name of education, the humanists in the system will continue to dominate them and force them to disseminate unsupported and unscientific dogma. *Academic freedom* in public education only means freedom to teach humanism.

The humanists will not even permit the school premises (paid for by taxpayers) to be used to teach anything Christian or biblical. What is the reason? They are afraid that an alternate view will reverse the brainwashing process before graduation day. True science, assured of its facts, welcomes alternate viewpoints, for truth is sharpened by exposure. Humanists know that their theories rest on unsupported propaganda, not scientific fact. That is why they become so emotional when confronted by a creation scientist who knows as much about evolution as they do—but doesn't believe it.

Currently, the humanists are becoming quite agitated about the success of the creationist movement in getting fair-minded school systems to insist that scientific creationism be taught along with the theory of evolution in our public schools. It is absolutely incredible how paranoid and emotional some Ph.D.s can get at the very thought of giving equal time to creation, the oldest and best model of origins. For thirty years, they have had it all their way, teaching only evolutionary theory. Being forced to give equal time to creation unnerves them. Legislators in the state of Georgia voted to require that creationism be taught along with evolution, as an alternate model for students to choose from. Parents favored it, taxpayers supported it, and the legislators ordered it. But who balked? The high priests of education, of course. They as much as told the legislators to keep their noses out of the education business. In recent years, that has been the response of educators when confronted by parents and others over such things as radical sex education, values clarification (or morals modification), unisex teachings, and creation. "Dole out money for good salaries and costly buildings, textbooks and educational services, and give us the minds of your children—but don't tell us how to teach them." The fact that their educational experiments have resulted in the drastically lowered achievement levels of our youth doesn't bother them, and they can't understand why parents are upset. The only arrogance that exceeds that of some educators is that of the Ayatollah Khomeini, and both are after the same thing—mind control.

Christianity = Science
Humanism = Chaos

The present chaos in secular education (the cost of education has increased eight times in twenty years, while the level of education has gone down) is the typical result of humanism. It is not only wrong and unscientific, but downright harmful. And the more influence humanism exercises upon our culture, the more chaos it will produce.

Paradoxically, the humanists have taught that Christianity is religion—in their words, "a myth." Humanism, of course, does not deal with myth, for it is dedicated to "facts." Consequently, humanists have divided all thought into two categories: the theological (or mythological) and the scientific. Since they do not rely on theology, they have decreed and widely disseminated the idea that Christians are unscientific, while they are scientific.

So thorough were the humanists in this tactic that, from the 1930s to the late 1950s, most Christians suffered from what I call a false intellectual inferiority complex. In actuality, Christians have been the pioneers of education in the Western world, particularly in America. However, Christian educators have invested themselves in humanitarian activities and the preaching of the gospel, while the humanists of the past 100 years have been working increasingly for mind control, by assuming command of our government, education, commerce, the media, and in some cases, liberal churches.

Only in the past twenty years have Christian men of science come out of the woodwork. They have founded several creationist organizations, such as the Creation Research Center, with over 600 members (as compared to only 170 signers of the *Humanist Manifesto*). Christian colleges have grown tremendously in the past three decades, and many of their scholars have gone on to secular graduate schools with such thorough undergraduate training in biblical truth that they have remained uncorrupted by humanist brainwashing.

This ground swell of Christian scholarship, which is antagonistic to humanism, has served as the catalyst for many new books, magazines, and movies that are exposing humanism for the fraud it really is. Such disclosures, generated and disseminated at a time when the theories of humanism are proving themselves to be socially chaotic, are creating a tidal wave of national concern that has frightened the humanists. They realize that if enough pro-moral, pro-American, and Christian citizens become informed of the danger implicit in their unscientific theories, they will be voted out of office and the real American people will regain their country and culture.

Humanists love to identify the great scientists of the past as either humanists or their forerunners. Particularly, they wish to claim credit for both the Age of Enlightenment and the scientific revolution. What they fail to point out is that the freethinkers, the forerunners of atheists and ultimately of the humanists themselves, were predominately in the theoretical and

abstract fields of philosophy, economics, humanities, and be-
havorial studies. Few of them will be found in the concrete
fields of true science.

The truth of the matter is that the advanced educational
level and technological revolution unique to the Western
world, until a few years ago, would never have occurred, had it
not been for the fact that the Industrial Revolution was shaped
predominantly by men who believed in God. That is important, because theistic scientists assumed a nature that was designed to follow dependable laws. Atheistic humanists, obsessed with unguided and continual change, would have had us
back in the Dark Ages, where they were still attempting to trial
and error their theories.

Dr. Francis Schaeffer points out that even many secular scientists acknowledge science's debt to Christianity—rather than
to humanistic theories:

> . . . indeed, at a crucial point the Scientific Revolution rested
> upon what the Bible teaches. Both Alfred North Whitehead
> (1861–1947) and J. Robert Oppenheimer (1904–1967) have
> stressed that modern science was born out of the Christian
> world view. Whitehead was a widely respected mathematician
> and philosopher, and Oppenheimer, after he became director
> of the Institute for Advanced Study at Princeton in 1947,
> wrote on a wide range of subjects related to science, in addi-
> tion to writing on his own field on the structure of the atom
> and atomic energy. As far as I know, neither of the two men
> were Christians or claimed to be Christians, yet both were
> straightforward in acknowledging that modern science was
> born out of the Christian world view.
>
> Oppenheimer, for example, described this in an article "On
> Science and Culture" in *Encounter* in October 1962. In the
> Harvard University Lowell Lectures entitled *Science and the
> Modern World* (1925), Whitehead said that Christianity is the
> mother of science because of "the medieval insistence on the
> rationality of God." Whitehead also spoke of confidence "in

the intelligible rationality of a personal being." He also says in these lectures that because of the rationality of God, the early scientists had an "inexpugnable belief that every detailed occurrence can be correlated with its antecedents in a perfectly definite manner, exemplifying general principles. Without this belief the incredible labors of scientists would be without hope." In other words, because the early scientists believed that the world was created by a reasonable God, they were not surprised to discover that people could find out something true about nature and the universe on the basis of reason.[84]

Dr. Schaeffer further clarifies that, while not all the scientists of the Age of Enlightenment were committed Christians, all lived in what he calls a Christian consensus. Consequently, their theories were heavily influenced by a universe of order and design, even if they personally did not believe in a Designer.

Living within the concept that the world was created by a reasonable God, scientists could move with confidence, expecting to be able to find out about the world by observation and experimentation. This was their epistemological base—the philosophical foundation with which they were sure they could know. (*Epistemology* is the theory of knowledge—how we know, or how we know we can know.) Since the world had been created by a reasonable God, they were not surprised to find a correlation between themselves as observers and the thing observed—that is, between subject and object. This base is normative to one functioning in the Christian framework, whether he is observing a chair or the molecules which make up the chair. Without this foundation, Western modern science would not have been born.

Here one must consider an important question: Did the work of the Renaissance play a part in the birth of modern science? Of course it did. More than that, the gradual intellectual and cultural awakenings in the Middle Ages also exerted their influence. The increased knowledge of Greek thought—at Padua University, for example—opened new doors. Certainly, Renaissance elements and those of the Greek intellectual traditions were involved in the scientific awakening. But to say theoretically that the Greek tradition would have been in itself a sufficient stimulus for the Scientific Revolution comes up against the fact that it was not. It was the Christian factor that made the difference. Whitehead and Oppenheimer are right. Christianity is the mother of modern science because it insists that the God who created the universe has revealed himself in the Bible to be the kind of God he is. Consequently, there is a sufficient basis for science to study the universe. Later, when the Christian base was lost, a tradition and momentum had been set in motion, and the pragmatic necessity of technology, and even control by the state, drives science on, but, as we shall see, with a subtle yet important change in emphasis.[85]

Men of Faith and Men of Science

Francis Bacon (1561–1626) is called by Dr. Schaeffer "the major prophet of the scientific revolution." A lawyer, essayist, and lord chancellor of England, he stressed careful observation and a systematic collection of information to unlock nature's secrets. He took the Bible seriously, including the historic Fall.[86]

Johannes Kepler (1571–1630), a German astronomer known as the father of modern astronomy, was the first to show that the planets' orbits are elliptical, not circular. His faith is clearly expressed in the preface of his book *The Mystery of the Universe:* "Since we astronomers are priests of the highest God in regard to the book of nature, it befits us to be thoughtful, not of the glory of our minds, but rather, above all else, of the glory of God."[87]

Robert Boyle (1627–1691), known as the father of modern

chemistry, was renowned for his careful observation. According to the *Encyclopaedia Britannica,* Boyle viewed nature as "a mechanism that had been made and set in motion by the Creator at the beginning and now functioned according to secondary laws, which could be studied by science."[88] He stressed that the scientific research "helped to reveal the greatness of the Creator."[89] Though a member of the Royal Society and a dedicated scientist, he was equally committed to propagating the Gospel abroad, translating the Scriptures into Irish and Turkish, and writing material on the harmony of his scientific and Christian positions. Even the endowment provided in his will for the Boyle lectures stipulated that they persist "for proving the Christian Religion against notorious infidels."[90]

Sir Isaac Newton (1642–1727) is famous for his discovery of the law of gravity. However, we often forget that he also invented calculus and in 1687 published *The Mathematical Principles of Natural Philosophy,* which became:

> ... one of the most influential books in the history of human thought. By experimenting in Neville's Court in Trinity College at Cambridge University, he was also able to work out the speed of sound by timing the interval between the sound of an object which he dropped, and the echo coming back to him from a known distance.

> Throughout his lifetime, Newton tried to be loyal to what he believed the Bible teaches. It has been said that seventeenth-century scientists limited themselves to the *how* without interest in the *why.* This is not true. Newton, like other early scientists, had no problem with the *why* because he began with the existence of a personal God who had created the universe.

> In his later years, Newton wrote more about the Bible than about science, though little was published. Humanists have said that they wish he had spent all of his time on his science. They think he wasted the hours he expended on biblical study, but they really are a bit blind when they say this. As White-

head and Oppenheimer stressed, if Newton and others had not had a biblical base, they would have had no base for their science at all.[91]

Blaise Pascal (1623–1662), a brilliant mathematician, invented the barometer and is considered by some a major writer of French prose.

> An outstanding Christian, he emphasized that he did not see people lost like specks of dust in the universe (which was now so much larger and more complicated than people had thought), for people—as unique—could comprehend something of the universe. People could comprehend the stars; the stars comprehend nothing. And besides this, for Pascal, people were special because Christ died on the cross for them.[92]

Michael Faraday (1791–1867) never had the benefit of formal education, yet he invented the electric transformer, motor, and generator. He developed the concept of electromagnetic fields. He engaged in experimental organic chemistry by separating benzene from heating oil. Faraday was a Christian who belonged to a small religious order that believed "the Bible, and that alone, with nothing added to it nor taken away from it by man, is the sole and sufficient guide for each individual, at all times and in all circumstances."[93] Faraday's scientific but thoroughly Christian search for truth was based upon faith in biblical creation and salvation through Jesus Christ.

James Clerk Maxwell (1831–1879), a physicist, is one of the most respected men of science. A man who extended Faraday's research in magnetic fields and electricity, he united the concept of force fields (forces acting through a distance) into a set of four equations. His electromagnetic theory was instrumental in advancing experimentation in optics and electronics. Raised in a Christian home, by eight years of age, "he had memorized all 176 verses of Psalm 119. Maxwell lived during the period of

Charles Darwin, when evolutionary faith was spreading rapidly. He saw through this counterfeit to true faith immediately, and opposed it."[94]

Space does not permit us to include the many other scientists of faith, such as Humphrey Davey, Samuel Morse, James Joule, William Thompson (Lord Kelvin), and the hundreds of competent men of science today who believe in a personal God of design and order and who reject the false claims of atheistic humanism and its brainchildren, evolution and amorality. (For additional information on the unscientific theory of evolution, write The Institute of Creation Research, 2100 Greenfield Drive, El Cajon, CA, 92021.)

All scientists have not been men of faith, but those who founded true scientific research were largely men of faith or those who were influenced in their thinking by the Christian consensus. The belief that God the Lawgiver has incorporated basic laws within His universe that are discoverable and dependable has contributed largely to the development of modern science. Not until what Dr. Schaeffer calls the age of "modern modern science" did a number of scientists begin to sink into skepticism, atheism, amorality, and socialism. In Europe, humanists gradually took over the educational system and fabricated a false science, built on the discoveries of men of faith in an orderly universe but attributing those findings to "change and change." Today the educational takeover by humanists makes it all but impossible for those untaught in the Bible to distinguish between true science and humanistic theory, for all are called scientific by the humanists. That is one of the main reasons they expelled the Bible from the public schools in 1957. Since then, it has become fashionable to teach our youth, in addition to unscientific humanism, such things as transcendental meditation (TM), the occult, witchcraft, and virtually anything students wish to study—except the Bible. Why? Because the Bible will expose humanism as a fraud. Nothing else will.

Humanism's Five Unscientific Basics

In chapter 3, we established the five basic tenents of humanism from their own prominent writers, and in chapter 4, we reviewed the religious precepts from their official bible, *Humanist Manifestos I and II.* Now we shall demonstrate that this religious belief, masquerading as science, is so fraudulent that *not one of its five basic tenets can be proved.* In fact, measurable statistics and evidence contravene humanistic doctrine.

Atheism   If a man came to town saying, "No one plus nothing, times blind chance, equals everything," we would say he was crazy, because he would expect us to believe that effect can be achieved without cause and design without a designer. But if he came to town displaying an academic degree and proclaimed, "Educated people do not believe in God. Instead, they believe that by chance this world evolved over millions of years, and we, like our animal brothers, are the product of spontaneous life," he is acclaimed a great thinker and called a humanist.

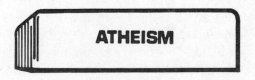

In actuality, neither the Christian nor the humanist can scientifically prove the existence or nonexistence of God. That is, the inductive method is useless in such an endeavor. The universe is so vast and so complex that it literally staggers the mind of all men, both humanist and Christian. Since God, if He exists, would of necessity have to be superior to His creation, He would essentially have to be greater than not only man, but all of His creation—the earth, the other planets, and the universe. He obviously is not discernible with the human eye, for then any controversy related to His existence would cease. Therefore, we conclude that it is impossible to prove empirically whether God exists—or does not exist.

Since the nonexistence of God is unprovable, it is unscientific to dogmatically deny that He exists—particularly when there is ample circumstantial evidence to the contrary.

Man does not have to verify things with his five senses, to conclude that they are real. Have you ever seen gravity, electricity, or love? Yet they exist, and their reality is provable by what they do. When we see light emanating from a bulb, we know that the electricity is on, although we have not observed it in its essential form. When a mother declares that she loves her baby, we cannot see her love. But when she throws her body in front of certain death to save the life of her child, we know, by what she does, that she loves.

So it is with God. We do not see Him, but we observe His works everywhere. The 120 trillion brain connections in your head loudly proclaim a Designer. The capillaries in your body, which, if laid end to end, would wrap five times around the earth, are in such synchronized working order that they carry blood, nutrition, and oxygen to your entire body. Did they get there by blind chance? Since we must accept either creation or evolution by faith, it seems more logical to believe that a Designer planned and created mankind. So it is with mountains, streams, stars, and everything in this world; they are effects that demand an Almighty cause.

Another bit of evidence we must consider in our attempt to validate the existence of God is the Bible: the oldest and most amazing book in the world. Written over a period of 1,600 years by more than 40 different people, it has a supernatural consistency about it. No other book has been so loved, so hated, so persecuted, or so used as the Bible. From beginning to end, it renders a persistent message: There is a God; He is the uncaused Cause of all things; And He loves man very much. Nineteen hundred years ago, this book was completed, never to be corrected or updated. Its pages contain many signs of the supernatural, such as hundreds of prophecies that have historically been fulfilled. Its archeological accuracy is acclaimed to be incredible. To those who have studied it carefully, it bears all the signs of what it claims—divine authorship.

If you hesitate to accept that bit of evidence, let's consider the alternative that the humanists have to offer. Their belief is relatively new—about 300 years old, as compared to over 6,000 years for the Scriptures. In 1933, they codified their first version of the humanist bible—*Humanist Manifesto I.* In 1973, they updated it and clearly stated that it was not complete but is open for future revision.

It would be hard for anyone to weigh both sides of the evidence and conclude with the humanists that there is no God. They cannot muster any scientific proof for His nonexistence to counterbalance the many evidences of His existence. They certainly cannot offer a single illustration to prove that anything has ever come into existence without a designer. The truth is, atheism is unscientific.

Evolution The biggest hoax of the nineteenth and twentieth centuries is that evolution is a scientific fact. Admittedly, it is a widely accepted *theory* of man's origin, held chiefly by those who reject a belief in God, but theories are not accepted as scientific fact until they can be proved. Remember, the hypothesis that traces man's lineage back to the amoeba has never been substantiated, and there is increasing evidence to the contrary. Not only do the 600 Creation Research Society scientists re-

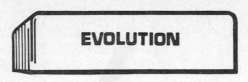

EVOLUTION

ferred to earlier reject the idea that evolution is a fact, but many nontheistic scientists admit to a startling lack of evidence. In chapter 4 we cited several sources, beginning with Thomas Huxley, who admitted that evolution was only a hypothesis. Dr. Clark acknowledged that there are no "missing links" and no substantial evidence for evolution.

Creation obviously occurred *before* anyone was around to witness the incident. Consequently, it is impossible to verify its occurrence by witnesses. In fact, the best evidence for evolution should appear in fossils embedded in rocks, but so many questions arise in this study (paleontology) that even many evolutionary paleontologists put little stock in the record of the rocks. Besides, all such formations can be accounted for by a universal flood, which both the Bible and modern archeology substantiate. Basing one's belief in evolution on geology or paleontology, therefore, can scarcely be considered scientific. Dr. Robert A. Millikan, a physicist and Nobel prize winner, stated in a speech before the American Chemical Society: "The pathetic thing about it is that many scientists are trying to prove the doctrine of evolution, which no science can do."

My first experience with evolution probably best illustrates why such an unscientific theory is accepted as fact by so many. In my junior-high-school biology textbook, I saw with my own eyes a picture of the missing link. As a matter of fact, I saw four of them: photographs of the Java man, the Piltdown man, *Pithecanthropus erectus,* and Peking man. These photos of manlike creatures really shook my faith in the Bible, which fulfilled the humanist intentions of the authors. (I have since discovered that for many humanists, truth is not "right" as opposed to "wrong," but whatever advances the humanist cause.) Subsequent research disclosed that all four of those missing links were frauds—nothing more than one or two bones or teeth of humans. Piltdown was just an ordinary ape bone. From these few particles, the scientists or educators made plaster-of-Paris models, photographed them and put them in our science textbooks. (For additional information on the hoaxes of the missing links, see Dr. Duane Gish's book, *The Fossils Say No*. Available through Institute for Creation Research, 2100 Greenfield Drive, El Cajon, CA 92021.) They fully did the work they were intended to do, brainwashing millions of children with the "scientific" theory of evolution. Is it any wonder that so many Americans believe that man descended from monkeys, even though not one scientific fact can prove such a distorted claim?

The humanists want us to believe that a great miracle (spontaneous life) happened millions of years ago and that life (contrary to any observable scientific evidence) developed into higher and higher forms, until man resulted. This is the "scientific" theory that causes them to think man will continue to get better and better in the future.

Evolutionists, then, want us to believe something that happened several million years ago—a biological accident, which man in his most technologically advanced laboratories cannot reproduce today. The process of evolution demands a miracle—in fact, several miracles. Dr. Richard Bliss, professor of biology and science education at Christian Heritage College, has asserted, "The miracles required to make evolution feasible are far greater in number and far harder to believe than the miracle of creation."[95] If it takes a miracle or miracles either way, it seems more scientific to believe that those miracles were performed by a Miracle Worker with infinite intelligence. After all, everyone acknowledges that the universe reveals infinite design.

The theory of evolution is based on faith, not fact. By contrast, science is the study of fact. Therefore, evolution is unscientific!

Amorality During my lifetime, the "new morality," as vigorously advanced by humanists has overturned centuries of moral values and virtually created a new life-style for millions of people, particularly those under thirty years of age. That is not to say that preceding generations were moral purists. I spent two years in the Air Force, including one year in Germany, so I know better. But back then, an adulterer or fornicator was *immoral.* Today's generation is *amoral.* What is the difference? Conscience.

AMORALITY

Only animals, prostitutes, and moral degenerates could "sleep around," "bed hop," or practice "free love" without feeling guilty about it, in past generations. But the new morality, spawned in the creative minds of the God-rejecting humanists, is presented as science. Since it appeals to the baser appetites of mankind, giving him clinical or academic approval to practice his urges and "guaranteeing" that there are no absolutes, it silences his conscience by education.

A human being whose conscience has been killed is amoral. Consequently, he is capable of performing like the animal he considers himself; that is, he can be inhumane. If you deem that an exaggeration, you have forgotten that the humanistic doctors and psychiatrists of the Third Reich advocated and practiced euthanasia (the killing off of those considered unfit to live) before Hitler made it state policy.[96] The Germans could easily practice genocide against the Jews, because they had made a practice of eliminating the weak, old, and unwanted in the name of euthanasia before 1940.

Consider abortion for a moment. Nothing shows the amoral influence of humanism on modern thought like the 1973 decision of the United States Supreme Court to legalize abortion. How could the majority of that august body of judges come to such a lowly evaluation of human life as to decide that the unborn is a nonperson? "Expert" (humanistic) medical opinion led these judges to make their decision. As Dr. C. Everett Koop noted at a Schaeffer seminar, "I find it hard to understand why biologists have no trouble recognizing life in worms, frogs, rats, and rabbits, but medical doctors have a difficult time determining when life begins in the highest form of life—human beings."

Since 1973, over *eight million* abortions have been performed in America. At this rate, we will soon have to apologize to Adolf Hitler.

Those who favor abortion-on-demand are not necessarily humanists, but they certainly have been influenced by humanism's inadequate view of human life. The Bible sets a premium on human life, as illustrated by the fact that God gave His only Son for mankind. Jesus told us that life was worth more than the whole world (Matthew 16:26). Therefore, anyone who favors abortion does not reflect a biblical view of life, but shows the influence of humanism on his thought process. Such individuals should not be in charge of our government, nor should they have access to the impressionable minds of our young. Anything that takes eight million lives can hardly be called scientific or humane.

Amorality leads to misery. The big lie of amoral humanists is that sexual promiscuity or any form of amorality leads to happiness. Self-gratification may lead to immediate pleasure, but

invariably it sacrifices the permanent on the altar of the immediate. The Bible teaches, "Happy is he that *hears* the word of
God and *keeps* it" (*see* Luke 11:28). History proves that to be
true. Greece, Rome, and eighteenth-century France were sexually free—liberated and "democratic"—but they destroyed
their own culture with their sin. Individually as well as nationally, fleshly self-indulgence breeds misery.

Lest you think it can't happen here, consider the December
30, 1979 United Press story in the *San Diego Union:* "High
school pupils find life empty, joyless, a study says." Young
people in "affluent U.S. suburbs view their lives as empty and
meaningless" and "get their pleasure from sex and drugs and
consider school 'unpaid labor.' " The main problem those
young people face is "a lack of meaning in their lives," said a
Rutgers University sociology professor, Dr. Ralph W. Lar-
kin.[97]

A survey I conducted of 3,400 Christian married people revealed the highest sexual-satisfaction level of any survey to
date. It also showed that those who were virgins at the time of
marriage registered a higher satisfaction level than those who
were not. Humanists teach just the opposite.

The response to my book *The Unhappy Gays* even surprised
me. My counseling of homosexuals had convinced me that
they were anything but gay, experiencing more loneliness and
heartache than normal people and sustaining a higher incidence of suicide. I expected to get quite a bit of hate mail—and
I have received some—but to my surprise, the homosexuals
themselves have responded favorably by ten to one. Only a
blind humanist will reject the fact that perversion leads to
wretchedness.

One man, the superintendent of a 14,000 acre park in one of
the nation's largest cities, read the book and shared with one of
my associates that the people in his park naturally congregated
into four groups: Hispanics, blacks, Caucasians, and homosex-

uals. His comment was quite revealing: "Through the years the only area from which we have to haul out the bodies of suicide victims is the homosexual section." One need not be a scientist to deduce that homosexuality does not produce happiness. It is really a shame that humanists can't be forced to take the responsibility for their faulty teaching that homosexuality is "gay" or "just as good as straight." This simply is not true—and it isn't scientific!

Sweden the miserable. Objective-minded observers are concerned that the humanists who run our federally controlled school system are not learning a lesson from Sweden. Back in the early 1960s, Sweden was presented as the ideal society—humanist, sexually liberated, and socialist. A number of our sex-education courses were modeled after theirs. Currently, reports from that former beautiful land of the Vikings reveal that it has the highest suicide rate in the world. VD and drunkenness are rampant, and the people have lost all hope for change.

A recent TV documentary presented an interview with several Swedish youth, none of whom expressed any interest in getting married, having children, or securing a job; none had any hope for the future. The despair of the elderly was appalling. In fact, interviews with both young and old made clear the common dread of growing old. Senior citizens who were interviewed acknowledged an endless struggle between another meaningless, boring day of life and the legal right to commit suicide. So much for the sexually liberated, socialistic paradise of Sweden.

We don't have to look to other countries, however, to refute the unscientific claims of humanism that amorality leads to happiness. All we have to do is ask the young men who are impotent due to venereal disease or the girls who underwent hysterectomies to save their lives from VD resulting from practicing free love. Or consider the report out of Ohio State

University that indicated the divorce rate was *higher* among couples that had lived together at least three years before marriage than among those who had not. Similar failures were chalked up by the humanist-inspired communal living and wife-swapping programs of a few years back. I can remember when the high priests of humanism actually suggested that children raised in communes were better off than those raised by only two parents. Somehow, those "scientific" suggestions, which proved ineffectual and even counterproductive, are barely whispered today.

The silence of sex educators on the dangers of VD to sexually active teens is not only unscientific but borders on the criminal. Dr. Rhoda L. Lorand, a practicing New York City psychotherapist with prestigious academic qualifications, has written an indictment of modern sex educators for their silence on the growing problem of cancer of the cervix among sexually promiscuous girls. In a paper entitled "The Betrayal of Youth"[98] she quoted prominent medical research pointing out the little-known fact that, at the same time HEW is pushing for contraception availability for children ten to fourteen without parental consent, doctors are discovering teenage promiscuity can increase a girl's vulnerability to cancer by as much as five times. Dr. Lorand stated:

> One does not have to be a religious fanatic to recognize nature's message; the vulnerable immature reproductive system of the pubescent and adolescent girls is at risk of being prematurely damaged by prematurely engaging in the adult sexual activity of coitus.
>
> Moreover, multiple partners do not appear to be part of nature's design for the human species, as research on males confirms. Promiscuous boys and men risk becoming cancer-carriers, giving cervical cancer to women. In 1966, Dr. Clyde E. Martin presented these findings in a paper entitled "Marital and Coital Factors in Cervical Cancer" at the annual meeting

of the American Public Health Association. Dr. Martin's research revealed that women whose husbands were involved in extramarital coitus showed a much higher incidence of cervical cancer than those whose husbands were faithful.[99]

Dr. Irving I. Kessler of Johns Hopkins found that "extramarital sexual practice by either the woman or her spouse is also associated with cervical cancer risk...."[100] The process is not as yet understood, but it is clear that promiscuity is the central factor. Venereal disease, once controlled, but for this generation a rapidly escalating menace, is a consequence of humanist propaganda.

Dr. Lorand added another interesting comment: "Other investigators have discovered that the disease is almost non-existent in nuns, whereas there is a high rate of cervical cancer in prostitutes."[101]

Evidently, morality is good for your health, whereas amorality can shorten your life span. If humanists are *really* objective scientists, why are they silent on this subject? Why don't they mount a serious campaign to warn teenagers that promiscuity leads to cancer?

The truth is, amorality does not promise a happy life. To claim otherwise is unscientific.

Autonomous, Self-Centered Man   All of the humanistic notions about man being autonomous, self-productive, and capable of solving his personal problems, as well as mankind's, independent of God are based on the unscientific principle that man is basically good by nature. As every Christian knows, that is contrary to biblical teaching: "... there is none good ..." (Mark 10:18). "All have sinned, and come short of the glory of God" (Romans 3:23). "The heart is deceitful ... and desperately wicked ..." (Jeremiah 17:9). Even Jesus began one of His commentaries, "If ye, then, being evil ..." (Matthew

7:11). The Bible consistently assumes the sinfulness of man due to the Fall. Humanists, however, repudiate the Fall and demand that man be granted godlike goodness.

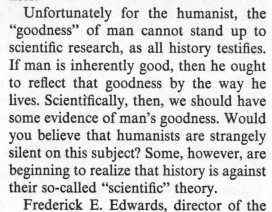

Unfortunately for the humanist, the "goodness" of man cannot stand up to scientific research, as all history testifies. If man is inherently good, then he ought to reflect that goodness by the way he lives. Scientifically, then, we should have some evidence of man's goodness. Would you believe that humanists are strangely silent on this subject? Some, however, are beginning to realize that history is against their so-called "scientific" theory.

Frederick E. Edwards, director of the California chapter of the American Humanist Association, said in a published interview in the *San Diego Evening Tribune:* "I have a fairly cut-and-dried approach I use to solve problems, although I realize it's not necessarily going to give me the right answer all the time. Humanists would decide abortion, euthanasia and other moral questions by saying an act is right or wrong, depending on its consequences." He then gave a typically humanistic idea on how to gain happiness: "What makes a man happy is the fulfillment of most of his needs."

To his credit, Edwards candidly admitted, "Humanists no longer have the extravagant faith they had in the 17th and 18th century Age of Enlightenment in man's ability to create a perfect world. I think cold, hard reality has thrown cold water on some of those naive illusions. We may be finding that our powers are limited and that we're not such perfectly wonderful creatures after all. . . ."

The best way to judge the quality of human nature is to examine what it does when it is free and unrestrained. History proves that unrestrained man has a natural penchant for criminality and inhumanity toward his fellowman. Consider the world's kings, presidents, dictators, or governors. In our "enlightened era," recall Joe Stalin, who caused over 30 million of his own countrymen to be put to death; or Mao Tse-tung, who killed an estimated 60 million Chinese people; or humanist Adolf Hitler; or even the presidents, vice-presidents, senators, congressmen, and governors in our own country who have proved to be less than honorable or have tried to elevate themselves above the law. Scientifically speaking, unrestrained man is an embarrassment to humanist ideals.

While on the subject, I must call attention to an interesting historical contrast. At the same time in history that Communist dictators were exterminating both friends and foes (the 1940s and 1950s), the United States, a nation born out of the Christian consensus of the Reformation, did something unparalleled in all of history. When we had Japan and Germany in a state of helpless, unconditional surrender, instead of enslaving them, as many might have done, we restored their freedom and rebuilt them, until today they are our two strongest economic competitors. Where did that kind of goodness come from? It certainly was not the result of humanism!

Even humanists admit that the strength of the United States form of government and its durability (the longest period of free elections of any country in history) is due to our unique checks and balances. That is, we do not have an autonomous president, Supreme Court, or legislature. Each is a check on the other. Where did that unique idea come from? It came from the understanding of our forefathers that human nature was not to be trusted and that man functions best when subjected to checks and balances. Our forefathers were not, of course, all Christians. But the Christian consensus of the day was so strong that they seriously acknowledged the fallen nature of man and designed history's greatest constitution around it.

Man tends to selfishness, not goodness; but only the humanists refuse to see that. One would think the reports coming out of Cambodia, South Vietnam, Uganda, and South Korea would convince the humanists. But just as they refused to heed the testimony of Dr. Tom Dooley that was written into the *Congressional Record,* of Chinese and North Korean Communist tortures that defy human comprehension, they refuse to concede that unrestrained man is notoriously inhumane.

Actually, the unscientific naiveté of the humanists seems incomprehensible to both Christians and other practically minded individuals. And the higher up in humanistic education they have gone, the more naive they seem to be.

Dr. James Kennedy, highly respected pastor of the largest Presbyterian church on our continent and president of Evangelism Explosion, reports a classic illustration. While finishing the work on his doctor of philosophy degree at New York State University, he attended his final course with fifteen other students. His peers were college deans, university professors, and high-school principals.

> One day the discussion came around to national defense and monies being spent on armament. . . . Seeing that there was no point of agreement I finally said to myself, "I will get a point in which everyone agrees, and then we can move on from there.
>
> "I assume that all of you would agree that there is some need for some national defense. That is, if we scrap all of our bombs, and all of our planes, and all of our ships, and tanks, and guns, and disbanded our army and navy and air force, I assume that you all would agree that it would be just a foot race to see whether Russia or China got to the Mississippi first."

Silence. "No, I don't agree with that," said one. "Nor I," said another. "Nor I," said a third and a fourth and a fifth. To my utter astonishment it turned out that there wasn't one single person in that classroom that felt that Russia or China or anyone else would move one little finger against us. They were convinced that the imperialism of America was the only cause of the trouble of the world today. And if we disarmed, it would simply usher in an era of universal peace. Now, that kind of reasoning is based on the concept that basically people are good.

You can see the political ramifications of that very unbiblical view of man. And even if you point out to some of these people that history clearly refutes that view, they still don't seem to be impressed.[102]

Most intelligent, pro-moral, pro-American citizens who read such an account can hardly believe that such Ph.D.s could be entrusted with the minds of our youth. Is it any wonder that so many defectors, deserters, and draft dodgers surfaced during the Vietnam conflict? Yet we pay the salaries of those educators. Interestingly enough, the higher up a person goes on the humanistic educational ladder, the more he thinks American capitalists are the real threat to world peace, not the peace-loving Communists. The working men and women of America are not confused—just their leaders.

Taken a step further, the humanist (in spite of all historical evidence to the contrary) has this strange concept about man's innate goodness: The poor are good—all they need is better housing, food, and money; the rich are bad, particularly capitalists; government leaders are good. Somehow the humanist mind conceives of government leaders as immune to temptation. That is why international gangsters and murderers like Joseph Stalin, Mao Tse-tung, Leonid Brezhnev and others are readily forgiven for their savagery and are respected as great world leaders.

An example of man's innate goodness was apparent for all to see on the evening news in the fall of 1979, during the destructive hurricane David, which stormed through several cities from Florida to Louisiana. In spite of the devastation and suffering experienced by the victims of David, "innately good" looters swept through the ruins to take advantage of the helpless. Interestingly enough, there was no looting in the Mississippi towns struck by the hurricane, because the governor, fully aware of human nature, called out the national guard. Humanist man failed again.

If man is in fact innately good, the humanist should be able to prove it. We are still awaiting his proof. Therefore, this point in humanist doctrine, like the others, is unscientific.

Socialist Success—Fact or Fable?   The most dangerous of the five basic tenets of humanism is their *theory* that a one-world, socialist state would solve all the problems of the world. It

taxes the credibility of intelligent people to understand how humanists can call this social experiment a science, when socialism has proven to be a classic failure in *every* area in which it has been tried (Russia, China, Eastern Europe, Africa, and Cuba). Socialism demotivates man and causes him to underproduce, plunging millions of people into a second-rate, despairing way of life.

I have visited five Communist countries: Czechoslovakia, Rumania, Poland, East Germany, and Soviet Russia. All are light years behind us, economically. They boast of full employment, and that's probably true, but I saw many government jobs in the places we visited (such as hotels) that had as many as three people doing one person's work. If a state-controlled economy is so superior, why after fifty years in "the worker's paradise" does only one family in fifty own a car? It's because the cost is equivalent to seven years of salary. Who in this country could afford an automobile, if he had to sacrifice his entire earnings for seven years to pay for it?

It is well-known that in Russia the peasants grow better and bigger crops on their tiny, privately owned gardens than are produced on the great, government-controlled cooperatives. This year the nation that under the czars was known as the breadbasket of Europe has to import millions of tons of wheat from America, just to feed its people.

State socialism has proved to be such a demotivating experience that even the Soviets have started to use some free-enterprise policies in an attempt to increase their productivity. The only people still enamored by socialism are the idealistic humanists, who have never lived under it.

One conservative economist, educated in the late 1960s and early 1970s, surprised me when I asked how he escaped the usual socialist, one-world view in his humanistic education. "I didn't," he replied. "I used to be a social liberal, but five years ago I took a three-week trip to Russia. That opened my eyes."

Perhaps we should send all Ph.D.s to Russia for three weeks, hoping for such a cure. Unfortunately, that trip would not arrest the tunnel vision of humanists, who doggedly preserve their unscientific obsession for world socialism. Corliss Lamont, one of the most influential of humanists, exalts over the "great political revolutions of modern times," including the French Revolution of 1789, the Russian Communist Revolution of 1917, and the anticolonial revolutions in Africa. He then says of them, "These tremendous mass upheavals have transformed much of the world and have had an immense impact throughout the globe. They have opened up new pathways to mankind's achievement of a truly Humanistic order."[103] To this we reply: Yes, they have resulted in the murder of between 100 and 120 *million* human beings. Africa today has 27 dictators, most of them ruthless and inhumane, although not as excessive as Idi Amin and ex-president Jomo Kenyatta. This man, remember, has served as a professor at Columbia University, teaching thousands of our educators, who in turn educate the teachers of our children. Is it any wonder that our young are being brainwashed regarding the glories of a one-world, socialist ideal? College students do not accept the thesis because it is grounded in fact, but because humanist educators say so.

Here is a simple test to prove that socialism has failed to provide the freedom, liberty, and prosperity that its humanist theorists have predicted for 200 years: How many are clamoring to gain citizenship in Communist countries? Rarely does anyone seek the welcome mats of the countries who feature the big armies, repress the people, and implement elaborate security systems to keep the people from escaping. If "the worker's paradise" is such a paradise, why doesn't it open its borders and let the people choose whether to stay or leave? Their leaders know the answer, and so do you.

Humanist-inspired socialism is a scientific failure! So is humanism.

7

Humanism Is a Religion

Only one organization in America can stop the complete "humanization" of our nation: the church of Jesus Christ. Unfortunately, the church seems apathetic in its response to humanism, possibly because the wolf has so neatly hidden beneath his woolly disguise. Knowledgeable Christians will rise up against religious heresy or a curtailment of basic freedoms, but their fighting instincts do not seem to be aroused by the terms *secular humanism* or *scientific humanism*. Even though the past decade has found humanists freely admitting the religious nature of their faith, many people are still under the delusion that it is a philosophy or an academic theory, and thus worthy of consideration in tax-supported educational institutions. Under the guise of philosophy, humanism has been granted a reputable position in American society.

The truth is, humanism is unmistakably and demonstrably a religion. The following nine facts will verify that thesis and, I hope, motivate you to oppose it vigorously in your city, state, and nation.

Humanists Call it a Religion

In the November-December, 1966, issue of the official organ of the American Humanist Association, *The Humanist,* appeared an article by the executive director, Tolbert H. McCarroll, entitled "Religions of the Future." He envisioned four major religions in the future, and he predicted that the one designated as "private humanism" would be "the largest religious body of the future."

Lloyd Morain, former president of the American Humanist Association, stated:

> Down through the ages men have been seeking a universal religion or way of life. . . . Humanism . . . *shows promise of becoming a great world faith.*
>
> Humanists are content with fixing their attention on this life and on this earth. *Theirs is a religion without a God,* divine revelation, or sacred scriptures (emphasis added).[104]

Another humanist leader, Edwin H. Wilson, observed:

> Many well-known thinkers have given voice to the hope of Religious Humanism that a comprehensive world religion will develop through the creative processes of our times. Roy Wood Sellars in 1927 held humanism to be the next step in religion. John Dewey, in his book *A Common Faith,* believed that we have all the materials available for such a faith. Sir Julian Huxley predicts that the next great religion of the world will be some form of humanism.[105]

The first official humanist organization in America was the Society for Ethical Culture, founded in 1876 by Felix Adler, a former rabbi and professor at Columbia University. Thirty additional societies were soon formed, and in 1889 Dr. Adler formed a national federation of these societies. In 1896, the Ethical Movement, or Humanist Movement, as it later came to be known, went international.[106]

The religious nature of this original humanist organization becomes evident in the following statement appearing in the November-December, 1964, issue of *Ethical Culture Today:*

Ethical Culture is listed as a religion in the Census of Religious Bodies published by the Federal Government, and in various religious publications and general reference works. Federal tax exemption rulings have been issued to the American Ethical Union and to the various Ethical Societies.[107]

In the March, 1978, issue of *Educational Leadership,* James K. Uphoff offered a broad definition of religion which " . . . envisions religion as any faith or set of values to which an individual or group gives ultimate loyalty . . . Ethical Culture, secularism, humanism, scientism . . . illustrate this concept of religion."[108]

Humanism is indeed a religion, and has been since its inception. During the last two decades or so, the humanists have come out of their closets and admitted it.

Humanist Bible Calls it a Religion

Nine times, the *Humanist Manifesto I* plainly calls its beliefs a religion. For instance: "Humanism is a philosophical, religious, and moral point of view as old as human civilization itself. It has its roots in classical China, Greece, and Rome; it is expressed in the Renaissance and the Enlightenment, in the scientific revolution, and in the twentieth century."[109]

Discarding traditional religion as having lost its significance and being "powerless to solve the problems of human living in the Twentieth Century," *Manifesto I* calls for "a break with the past" and the establishment of a "vital, fearless, and frank religion capable of furnishing adequate goals and personal satisfactions." Naturally, that religion is humanism. The manifesto then lays out fifteen affirmatives as tenets of its religion, concluding with the words, "So stand the theses of religious humanism."

Manifesto II makes it clear that man serves as God: " ... as non-theists we begin with humans not God, nature not deity." After affirming its faith in evolution, the declaration of faith goes on to bluntly state, "No Deity will save us; we must save ourselves."

Calling traditional religions an obstacle to human progress, this manifesto, which rejects the revelation of God in the Scriptures, speaks with an authority that comes either from an all-knowing deity or an all-consuming ego—and that is what humanism really is: human ego and intelligence gone mad.

United States Supreme Court Calls it a Religion

Humanism has been favored by the Supreme Court during the past three decades. Not until 1961, however, was it recognized officially as a religion. Corliss Lamont describes the famous *Torcaso* v. *Watkins* case from the humanist perspective:

> In 1961 the U.S. Supreme Court took official cognizance of religious Humanism in the case of Roy R. Torcaso, a Humanist who was refused his commission as a Notary Public under a Maryland law requiring all public officers in the State to profess belief in God. In delivering the unanimous opinion of the Court that this statue was unconstitutional under the First Amendment, Justice Hugo L. Black observed: "Among religions in this country which do not teach what would generally be considered a belief in the existence of God are Buddhism, Taoism, Ethical Culture, Secular Humanism and others."[110]

The *Texas Tech Law Review* states that, "The *Seeger* decision defined religion as all sincere beliefs based upon a power or being or upon a faith, to which all else is subordinate or upon which all else is ultimately dependent." Thus, according to *Seeger,* religion "includes atheists, agnostics, as well as adherents to traditional theism."

Such court decisions may account for Webster's 1970 dictionary definition of *religion,* which includes "any system of belief, practices, ethical values, etc., resembling, suggestive of, or likened to such a system [humanism as a religion]."

In the *Texas Tech Law Review,* attorney John W. Whitehead and former Congressman John Conlan published a lengthy article entitled "The Establishment of the Religion of Secular Humanism and Its First Amendment Implications." These lawyers cited several court decisions that have ruled or referred to humanism as a religion. For example, "One Federal Court in *Reed* v. *Van Hoven* has held that 'in light of the decided cases, the public schools, as between theistic and humanistic religions, must carefully avoid any program of indoctrination in ultimate values.' "[111] Obviously this judge equated theism and humanism as religions.

Referring to the 1965 Seeger case already mentioned, Whitehead and Conlan state, "The *Seeger* decision defined religion as all sincere beliefs 'based upon a power or being, or upon a faith, to which all else is subordinate or upon which all else is ultimately dependent.' Thus according to *Seeger,* religion includes atheists and agnostics, as well as adherents to traditional theism."[112]

Thomas Jefferson Calls Unbelief a Religion

We tend to think belief in God is a religion, and therefore disbelief is not a religion. The humanists have used that mistaken line of reasoning to the hilt! Actually, it is more accurate to say that one's view of God is a religious belief. As we have seen, atheism is unscientific, since it cannot be proven; consequently, all atheists *believe* in atheism.

Thomas Jefferson, writer of the Declaration of Independence, clearly understood this. During the debates that focused upon the separation of church and state, which ultimately led to the First Amendment, he defined the term *religion* to include "all believers or unbelievers of the Bible. . . ." This principle applies equally to believers or unbelievers in God.

By using our faulty thinking against us, religious humanists have labeled their doctrine *secular humanism,* ours *religion.* Then by claiming that morals originated with the teachers of the Bible, they, too, are classified as religious. Thus both religion and morality are excluded from our public schools, leaving them wide open to the religious doctrines of atheism; evolution; amorality; autonomous, self-centered man; and a socialist one-world view.

Using Thomas Jefferson's thesis, I would suggest that if belief and its biblical moral values are expelled from our public schools, so also should we expel humanist unbelief and its resultant amorality.

Humanism Has a Religious Theology

All religions are based on doctrinal teachings (or theology) that relate to God, origins, man, values, and the future life. As we have seen, humanism has constructed a well-defined theology:

- Disbelief in God
- Belief in evolution
- Rejection of absolute morals
- Deification of man as supreme
- Belief in the innate goodness of men to govern the world equitably

The theological position of humanism is so well-defined and established that if it were expelled from our public schools and its disciples were retired from government service through the ballot box, they would immediately declare themselves officially a religion and file as a tax-exempt religious organization. They cannot do so now because they receive over 140 billion dollars annually to operate their vast network of churches, called schools, colleges, and universities. Why should they collect donations to support the propagation of their religion when, through our taxes, we pay for their services? Parents are compelled to send their impressionable children to schools where, in the name of academic freedom, only the religion of humanism can be taught.

Whitehead and Conlan describe the issue in these words:

> . . .while Secular Humanism is nontheistic, it is religious because it directs itself toward religious beliefs and practices, that are in active opposition to traditional theism. Humanism is a doctrine centered solely on human interests or values. Therefore, humanism deifies Man collectively and individually, whereas theism worships God. Moreover, while humanism draws its values and absolutes from the finite reasoning or relativistic Man, theism has received its values and absolutes through the revelation of the infinite Deity or Creator. Both humanism and theism worship their own "god." The difference is the object of worship not the act. Therefore, Secular Humanism is a religion whose doctrine worships Man as the source of all knowledge and truth, whereas theism worships God as the source of all knowledge and truth.[113]

Humanism Must Be Accepted by Faith!

Christians have never hidden the fact that its followers accept its teachings by faith. This is not done blindly or irrationally, as the humanists often accuse. Our faith is the result of our using our mind, will, and heart in response to the revelation God has provided us in the Bible. That is what God meant, when He said through the prophet, "Come now, and let us reason together, saith the Lord . . ." (Isaiah 1:18). Faith comes by hearing the Word of God.

The humanist religion is likewise accepted purely by faith.

We have already established the fact that each of its five basic doctrines must be received by faith. For example, Corliss Lamont, whom many consider the clearest writer on humanistic thought (which is why I have quoted him so frequently), concludes his entire book with these words: "For his great achievements man, utilizing the resources and the laws of Nature, yet without Divine aid, can take full credit. Similarly, for his shortcomings he must take full responsibility. Humanism assigns to man nothing less than the task of being his own saviour and redeemer."[114] That concept, like every other in humanism, is totally unprovable and thus must be accepted by faith.

Christianity is a religious belief based on faith. So is Muhammadanism, Confucianism, and every other religion in the world.

Humanism is simply another religion of faith.

Humanism Is Rooted in Religion

We have already seen that modern humanism began with the Greeks (four centuries before Christ), all but vanished after the fall of Rome, and was revived by Saint Thomas Aquinas in the twelfth century. Both secular and Christian scholars agree on this.

But did these humanistic ideas originate with the Greeks? Hardly! They were a superstitious, polytheistic people, whose religion permeated their thinking, but even they didn't originate these ideas, for such teachings can be traced back to Confucius, Buddha, and even Babylon, the source of all religions. Even Lamont acknowledges the Greek (polytheistic) origin of humanism and then states that in the Orient, it found its way into the teachings of Confucius in China and Buddha in India.[115] As we have already noted, *Humanist Manifesto I* begins: "Humanism is a philosophical, religious, and moral point of view as old as civilization itself. It has its roots in classical China, Greece and Rome."[116]

Since humanists themselves freely admit their teachings originated in pagan religions, we may logically conclude that humanism is a religion, particularly in that it has maintained many of the same concepts found in these ancient religions.

This should dispel the notion among Christian thinkers that there are three kinds of thoughts prevalent today: two religious and one philosophical.

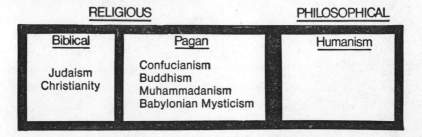

It is more accurate to postulate two kinds of religions today:

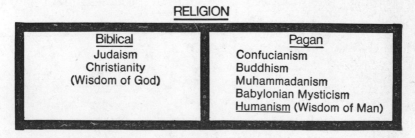

It should be obvious that since humanism originated in the ancient religions of man, still retains many of these beliefs, and is so compatible philosophically, even today, with these same religions, humanism, too, is a religion.

Unitarianism: The Source of American Humanism Unitarianism has done more to advance the humanist cause in America than any other organization. Unitarianism broke with Christianity over the essential deity of Jesus Christ. Like humanists, Unitarians believe Jesus to be human in every way, and both use Him as an ideal example of the humanist man.

Unitarianism, which gained prominence in Europe due to its liberal view of God, reducing Him to a deistic and impersonal Source of all things, became fertile ground for humanism. Both believed in the autonomy and self-sufficiency of man, who served as captain of his own fate. Many Unitarian humanists inhabited America during the eighteenth century, but it was not until 1825 that the Unitarians formally broke away from the Congregational Church and founded their own church. Many of the leading Unitarians today are also numbered as leaders of the humanist movement, and some have belonged to the same Ethical Cultural Societies. When *Humanist Manifesto I* was written 25 percent of its signers were Unitarians; 70 of the *Humanist Manifesto II* signers were Unitarians.[117] Lamont also cites a sermon preached in 1925 by the Reverend John H. Dietrich, who "showed how Unitarianism had naturally laid the basis for Humanism."[118]

By the twentieth century, the liberal spirit of higher criticism had so influenced Unitarianism that its members' deistic belief was hardly discernible from the humanist position. Unitarianism can be adjudged at least 95 percent humanistic, for it accepts four of the doctrines of humanism—evolution, amorality, autonomy, and a socialist one-world view. The difference between being a deist or an atheist is all that separates them from being 100 percent humanist. In other words, a Unitarian Sunday-school teacher can promote over 95 percent of his religious beliefs in the public school, by labeling them "education" or "secular humanism" or "scientific humanism," and get paid for it, Monday through Friday. That has to be the religious fraud of the century!

Humanism Is a Way of Life

The early Christians were often called followers of the way, because their religious beliefs caused them to practice a particular way of life. So it is with humanism.

One leading humanist, Lloyd Morain, claimed that humanism had doubled in each of the last few years. He then went on to point out that an increased number of Protestants, Jews, and Catholics were beginning to follow this "way of life." The humanistic path of life advocates a self-centered existence, independent of a personal God. Christianity, on the other hand, places its disciples in a position of being totally dependent upon God. Does not the fact that humanism is a way of life—just like any other religion—lend further credence to the fact that it can be classified as such?

Humanism Inspires Missionary Zeal

Dr. Mary Calderone, leading humanist and radical sex-education advocate, at seventy years of age travels over 100,000 miles a year to preach the humanist gospel—and she has done so for years. I can personally appreciate the toll that takes on a person, for I have traveled approximately that same amount annually for nine years, conducting Family Life Seminars based on biblical principles that strengthen family life. What makes hundreds of humanists run like this? It is a missionary zeal to propagate their humanistic religion.

Dr. James M. Parsons, a Florida psychiatrist, supplied an important missing piece to the puzzle of the humanist's religious procedure. For years I could not understand why individuals with Ph.D. degrees would spend their lives traveling the country, teaching permissive sex to anyone who would listen, until they had reduced lovemaking with a life partner to sexual activity with anyone. It didn't make sense! What did they have to gain? Dr. Parsons certified, "They are trying to create such an obsession with sex among our young people that they have no time or interest in spiritual pursuits."[119]

That explanation really fits, not only accounting for the humanists' radical sex-education policy but explaining why these educators inundate the minds of our youth with humanistic theology from kindergarten through college, teaching them that marijuana is not harmful (scientific evidence and reports notwithstanding); encouraging the use of drugs; advocating the freedom to use pornographic magazines (and, in some cases, assigning pornographic literature in place of the classics); ridiculing the values of their parents and the free-enterprise system; downgrading patriotism, and creating an obsession with everything but a quality education.

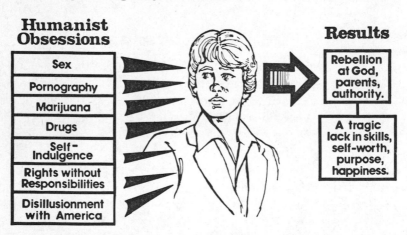

Their dedication can easily be explained when we understand that humanism is a religion and that its educational high priests are driven with a missionary zeal. The true nature of the process has only become recognizable during the past two decades, but it has really been operating in this country since the 1920s. The only subject upon which I am in agreement with humanists is that "John Dewey was the most influential educator of the twentieth century." He was truly the great, high priest of twentieth-century humanism. He and his disciples have taken over the public schools and turned them into tax-supported religious shrines that waste the potential of our young.

As in Jonesville, the youth of America are being mentally poisoned, so they will subjugate their minds, hearts, and wills to the elite high priests of education, their disciples in government, and the media, in preparation for the Orwellian Big Brother complex, which will enable the elite humanists to merge America with the Soviet Union and all other countries. This will culminate in the humanist dream of a one-world, socialist state.

Until the masses of America realize that humanism is a religion, not just a philosophy, the humanists will continue the "humanization" of our land. Once it is identified as a dangerous religion and expelled legally from our public schools, it will collapse under its own weight, for the American people—particularly parents—will never agree to subsidize the spiritual destruction of their children.

It is time that the 110,000 faithful ministers from every Bible-believing denomination in our country lead the 60 million Christians to vote out of office every devotee of humanism and every politician naive enough to vote for humanist programs. For example, every officeholder in our land—local, state, and national—regardless of party, who votes for or advocates the following, should be voted out of office:

• Abortion-on-demand
• Equal Rights Amendment

- Decriminalization of prostitution
- Approval of homosexuality and lesbianism
- Leniency on pornography
- Child's rights over parents' rights
- Legalizing of marijuana
- Gambling
- National weakness through disarmament

If the majority of Americans, whether religious or not, favor a pro-moral society in which to raise their family, they will replace humanized thinkers in government. Then laws can be passed that will safeguard the moral fiber of our land and return our nation to its former status as the most powerful nation on earth.

It has taken only thirty years to reduce our nation to moral degeneracy, national impotence, and economic inflation. If Christians and other pro-moralists worked together, we could return it to moral sanity in ten to fifteen years. What will be the result, if we refuse? the humanization and consequently the soul destruction of 50 million young people in each succeeding generation.

You may wonder why a minister and Christian educator for over thirty years opposes humanism so vigorously. There are two reasons: I am a committed Christian, and I am a committed American. Humanism is viciously opposed to both. Besides, I am commanded to warn the children of God when danger lies ahead. God told Ezekiel, ". . . if thou dost not speak to warn the wicked from his way, that wicked man shall die in his iniquity; but his blood will I require at thine hand" (Ezekiel 33:8).

The only reason more ministers are not warning their people of the dangers of humanism is they do not understand it. I hope by reading this book and others in my recommended bibliography, they will recognize humanism for what it is—a very dangerous religion.

The inability of many Christian leaders to understand the dangers of religious humanism can best be illustrated by an astonishing experience I had on January 22, 1980. Twelve ministers, most of whom are leading TV and radio preachers, were invited to have breakfast with the president. For fifty minutes he answered six questions, mainly on family living, morals, and national defense, all of which had been submitted in advance. The last one was, to me, the most revealing.

We asked, "Mr. President, in view of the fact that at least twenty percent of the American people are Christians, why is it that in the first three years of your administration you have not appointed one visible Christian to your cabinet—a judgeship or other high level of government?" He paused momentarily and then denied that this was the case. "I have several religious people in my administration," he explained. "... Vice-President Mondale is a very religious man and came from a very religious family. His father was a minister, his father before him was a minister, and his brother is a minister."

What the president said is true, but what he did not say is that Vice-President Mondale is a self-acknowledged humanist. Attorneys Whitehead and Conlan point out that:

> Vice-President Mondale, who has in the past been a contributor to *The Humanist,* was a major participant in the 5th Congress of the International Humanist and Ethical Union held at the Massachusetts Institute of Technology in August 1970. In his opening remarks, Mondale made the following comment:
> "Although I have never formally joined a humanist society, I think I am a member by inheritance. My preacher father was a humanist—in Minnesota they call them Farmer Laborites and I grew up on a very rich diet of humanism from him. All of our family has been deeply influenced by this tradition including my brother Lester, a Unitarian Minister, Ethical Culture Leader, and Chairman of the Fellowship of Religious Humanists."[120]

That visit to the White House further convinced me that this book is sorely needed. If the president of the United States does not understand that humanism and its grandfather, Unitarianism, are the unalterable foes of Christianity, then someone needs to unmask this false religion and expose its deadly doctrines and practices.

Homer Duncan is right, when he calls it the most dangerous religion in America.

8

Humanists Control America

America is supposed to be a free country, but are we really free? We are not free to turn on TV and find it unshackled

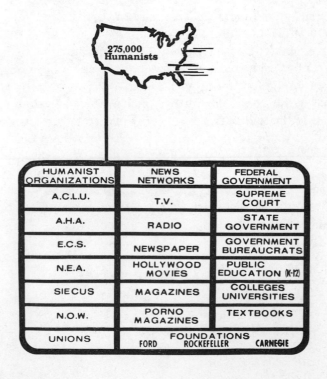

HUMANIST ORGANIZATIONS	NEWS NETWORKS	FEDERAL GOVERNMENT
A.C.L.U.	T.V.	SUPREME COURT
A.H.A.	RADIO	STATE GOVERNMENT
E.C.S.	NEWSPAPER	GOVERNMENT BUREAUCRATS
N.E.A.	HOLLYWOOD MOVIES	PUBLIC EDUCATION (K-12)
SIECUS	MAGAZINES	COLLEGES UNIVERSITIES
N.O.W.	PORNO MAGAZINES	TEXTBOOKS
UNIONS	FOUNDATIONS FORD ROCKEFELLER CARNEGIE	

from antimoral, prohumanist thinking, for humanists literally control the TV networks. We are not free to send our children to a school where they are safe from violence, drugs, and anti-American teachers. In fact, to provide our young with a high-caliber education that includes an emphasis on basics and character building, we must pay tuition to send them to a Christian school or other private school—while paying taxes to subsidize the religion of humanism in our public schools.

A free country, where the government is "of the people and by the people," should elect government leaders who are responsive to their constituency. Ours are not. For example, polls showed that 80 percent of the American people objected to the giveaway of the Panama Canal; yet our politicians gave it away. Consider abortion-on-demand, legalization of homosexual rights, government deficit spending, the size and power of big government, elimination of capital punishment, national disarmament, increased taxes, women in combat, passage of ERA, unnecessary busing, *ad infinitum.* If such measures were debated and voted upon by the people, they would be turned down; yet the politicians blithely enact legislation that is antithetical to the will of the majority. Have you ever asked why? It is all very simple, if you face the fact that we are being controlled by a small but very influential cadre of committed humanists, who are determined to turn traditionally moral-minded America into an amoral, humanist country. Oh, they don't call it humanist. They label it *democracy,* but they mean humanism, in all its atheistic, amoral depravity.

Degeneracy by Design

Many years ago, my mother, along with others of her generation, used to lament the rapid decline of morality in America. She considered the natural descent of fallen, secular man an irreversible trend. No doubt she echoed the feeling of most active Christians of her time.

What her generation did not realize was that the majority of Americans were not really that immoral by nature, but were being led down the path of moral degeneracy by the humanist social planners who dominated our society. A typical example is the widespread distribution of pornography. In my mother's youth, it was all but impossible to purchase hard-core pornography. Today it comes through the mail (often whether one wants it or not) or is otherwise so accessible that any schoolchild can peruse it, if he desires. Why such a change, in just fifty years? The American Civil Liberties Union has, for over half a century, busied itself by harassing our city councils, county boards of supervisors, legislators, courts, and ultimately the supreme courts of states and the United States, until they have finally destroyed the effective laws that would protect innocent eyes from the prurient use of the printed page. Today, actual photographs of every form of immoral, perverted, and even masochistic acts are readily available in livid color. No wonder we encounter so many bizarre sex crimes against mankind. Who is to blame? The humanist controllers of the American Civil Liberties Union and their humanist partners in moral crime—the judges who were appointed by the humanist politicians. Any morally minded citizen recognizes what the humanist refuses to admit: The free use of pornography increases immorality and sex crimes.

In the name of free speech and human rights, the humanists have plied their twisted logic before government leaders and fellow humanists in the courts, who for the most part agree with them. Never do they mention the human rights of parents to raise their children in a morally sane society. Indifferent toward parents, they intend to amoralize the young. All they want from us is our taxes, so they can go on living high at our expense, leading our country down the road to a socialist

Sodom and Gomorrah. They are so obsessed with the notion that biblical morality is a repressive system that they work untiringly to keep parents from injecting any moral ideals into their children. Believe it or not, their goal is a worldwide generation of young people with a completely amoral (or animal) mentality.

This incredible objective is the natural result of their belief in the unscientific theory of evolution. As committed evolutionists, they believe that man is an animal and, like the animals, should be free to satisfy the appetites of his glands. Biblical morality is to them the historic deterrent to self-actualized man living for the satisfaction of his glands. That is one of the reasons humanists have worked tirelessly in America, for over 150 years, to strike down every moral law of the land.

If you think that extreme, consider the following statements on freedom of expression, by Dr. Corliss Lamont:

> The Humanist stress on complete cultural democracy and freedom of expression means that artists and writers should have the widest latitude in what they produce and say. A free art and a free literature are absolute essentials for a free culture. . . .[121] Narrowly moralistic restraints on artists and writers have ever been a bane in the history of the West; and those restraints have frequently stemmed from the supernaturalist's suspicion of earthly pleasures. . . . The history of censorship in the fine arts, if it could be told in full, would be found to revolve in no small measure around the assumed peril of corruption of the spirit by the incitements of the flesh through beautiful things.[122]

This kind of justification for freedom of expression or freedom of speech, which the humanists have subtlely expanded to "freedom to read," is the reason that widespread pornography is forced upon us against our will. Many community surveys indicate that most Americans are opposed to pornography. Yet it still haunts us. Why? The humanists have decreed it so!

And what has this social experiment in producing a "better humanist world" accomplished? The same result produced by all their unfounded theories: chaos. The incidence of rape has doubled in the last decade. Homosexuality has run wild, resulting in mass murders unprecedented in American history (twenty-two trash-bag victims in California, thirty-four victims in Chicago, eighteen victims in Houston). An incredible increase in promiscuity, premarital sex, trial marriages, VD, abortions, and so forth has soiled our social fabric. These immoral expressions of amorality can scarcely be blamed on Christianity and biblical morality. But they can be laid right at the door of the atheistic, amoral humanism that permeates our country.

Until enough morally minded Americans understand what has taken place in the past few decades, the humanists will continue leading us toward the chaos of the French Revolution; after all, it was that same philosophy that destroyed France and paved the way for the dictator Napoleon Bonaparte. This time, the humanists hope to name their own dictator, who will create—out of the ashes of our pro-moral republic—a humanist utopia: an atheistic, socialistic, amoral humanist society for America and the rest of the world. In fact, their goal is to accomplish that takeover by or before the year 2,000. Consider Dr. Lamont's statement:

> Humanism takes the long view and remains hopeful of the decades to come. This philosophy, with its faith in man and in his ability to solve his problems through human intelligence and scientific techniques, holds to what might be called a reasoned optimism. It rejects the dead ends of despair as well as the daydreams of Utopia. I believe firmly that man, who has shown himself to be a very tough animal, has the best part of his career still before him. And there is at least the possibility that by the close of this century "the Humanist breakthrough," in Sir Julian Huxley's phrase, will spread throughout the globe to create a higher civilization of world dimensions.[123]

Dr. Kenneth Galbraith, an anti-free-economy expert and longtime humanist spokesman, has suggested plans for that humanist breakthrough are already underway, for he revealed an "elite," composed of intellectuals (especially the academic and scientific world) plus the government:

In June 1975, 2,000 "futurists" met for the Second General Assembly of the World Future Society in Washington, D.C. Socioeconomist Robert Theobald (1929–) endorsed the concept of "sapientary authority," a social structure in which wise men selected by merit would be deeply involved in the governmental decision-making process. "It's naive," declared Theobald, "to deny the necessity for some kind of competent elite."

Daniel Bell (1919–), professor of sociology at Harvard University, sees an elite composed of select intellectuals. He writes in *The Coming of Post-Industrial Society* (*1973*), in the chapter entitled "Who Will Rule," that "the university—or some other knowledge institute—will become the central institution of the next hundred years because of its role as the new source of innovation and knowledge." He says that crucial decisions will come from government, but more and more the decisions of both business and government will be predicated on government-sponsored research, and "because of the intricately linked nature of their consequences, [the decisions] will have an increasingly technical character." Society thus turns into a technocracy where "the determining influence belongs to technicians of the administration and of the economy." Bell sees that in the final analysis the whole state—its business, its education, its government, even the daily pattern of the ordinary man's life—becomes a matter of control by the technocratic elite. They are the only ones who know how to run the complicated machinery of society and they will then, in collusion with the government elite, have all the power necessary to manage it.

Bell's most astute warning concerns the ethical implications of this situation: "A post-industrial society cannot provide a transcendent ethic. . . . The lack of a rooted moral belief system is the cultural contradiction of the society, the deepest challenge to its survival." He adds that in the future men can be remade, their behavior conditioned, or their consciousness altered. The constraints of the past vanish. To the extent that Bell's picture of this future is fulfilled, Galbraith's form of the elite will be the actuality.[124]

Although the humanist elite, as Schaeffer calls them, are determined to turn America into an amoral, humanist, socialist state similar to Russia, *it is not inevitable*. We still have one good decade (perhaps two) to turn back the tide to traditional moral values and freedom for the individual. But it is imperative that we understand how the humanists have gained such mind control that only a few thousand of them can literally govern 216 million people. Interestingly enough, the same resources they have used during the last 100 years are still open to *us*. If a sufficient number of dedicated Christians and other pro-moral Americans use their influence, energy, and resources, we can return the humanists to private life and replace them with those who truly represent our nation and its best interests.

The Four Vehicles of Mind Control

When the humanists came to America, their obstacles seemed overwhelming. But rather than waste their resources, they concentrated on using four vehicles to penetrate the minds and lives of our people: education, the media, organizations, and government.

The Media We have already seen how John Dewey and his fellow humanists took over education and turned a once-safe and respected profession into a battle zone in which parents are increasingly becoming disenchanted with the educators' obsession to teach the religion of amoral humanism at the expense of a quality education. We have not mentioned, however, that other humanists were busy working their way into the media, controlling not only how Johnnie reads and sees but, to a large extent, *what* he reads and sees.

Space does not permit a detailed account of how newspapers from coast to coast were gradually purchased by powerful, monied interests. As radio came into view, it was bought up by some of these same interests. Later, when TV licenses became available, the humanists flooded the field. Today, it is all humanistically controlled, with only two wire services for newspapers and only three major TV networks.

Even though a newspaper is privately owned, it is dependent on the two wire services (Associated Press and United Press International) for its daily source of world and national news. This news is carefully edited before being sent out to the daily papers. Who does the editing? Who hired the editors, and what are their beliefs? Anyone really familiar with humanism can recognize its influence in the way the news is managed. Remember, a reporter cannot possibly report everything that is said or done. He must edit it down to what *he* thinks is important. If he is a humanist, what he considers important is inevitably colored by his humanistic outlook. If one of his favored politicians says something wrong or harmful to his image, that statement can be edited. If, however, a politician representing traditional moral values or economics makes a misstatement that can put him in a bad light, it hits the front page of every paper in the country.

An example of a newspaper cover-up is the coverage given President John Kennedy. The moral indiscretions of President Kennedy that have come to light in the past few years were well-known to Washington news reporters while he lived in the White House. But since humanists see nothing wrong with infidelity, they carefully sidestepped the truth. President Nixon, however, was relentlessly exposed by the newspapers—and rightfully so—for his wrongdoing.

The humanist wire services frequently show their bias in photographs. They rarely depict a liberal, humanist politician with his mouth open or in an uncomplimentary pose; but have you ever noticed how they photograph Mrs. Phyllis Schlafly, an attractive, articulate, conservative lawyer who opposes the ERA? They try their best to make a woman who is desperately trying to save America's families from the most dangerous amendment in history appear like a fanatic.

A classic example of the humanistic interpretation of events appeared recently in the November 25, 1979, issue of *Parade* magazine, the supplement in many Sunday newspapers around the country. The lead article, entitled "Public School Book Censors Try It Again," showed some people standing around a bonfire. The title may arouse memories of Nazi storm troopers or Communist KGB agents trying to control the reading of their citizens! This time, however, it was the story of two humble and very dedicated Christian patriots named Mel and Norma Gabler, who study modern textbooks and point out those teachings that are un-American or contrary to traditional moral values, or twist history and make unfair presentations of the free-enterprise system. Their textbook evaluations are printed and sent to parent groups in all fifty states. The writer of the article would label this "censorship" but would probably deny that a purely humanistic education is mind control. In other words, it is not censorship to remove traditional moral values, and it isn't mind control to teach humanism exclusively.

Other evidence that we do not have a free and independent press in the United States, representing the majority feelings of the people, occurred in November of 1979. As predicted in the October 29 issue of *TIME,* thirty-three major magazines throughout the country bombed their readers with stirring challenges and stories to brainwash the American people on the need to pass the Equal Rights Amendment, even though the seven-year period has elapsed and we are in the midst of an unlegal extension period. The NOW convention in Los Angeles confided to its delegates that such a program was going to be launched and, true to their word, thirty-three magazines fell into place. All thirty-three magazines advocated the erroneous idea that passage of ERA would insure equal job opportunities for women. Of course, they neglected to release the harmful effects of the ERA amendment. The following examples are taken from a Concerned Women for America newsletter:

> Under Colorado law, a wife now shares equally in the obligation to support her family (under pain of criminal conviction of a class-five felony). This is what equality means—no longer is it a crime in Colorado for a husband to abandon his wife.
>
> In an ongoing marriage in Pennsylvania, under state ERA, a wife is now obligated to pay her husband's bills.
>
> In Delaware County, Pennsylvania, Common Pleas Judge William Tool said women must make support payments to husbands for children in their custody.
>
> In Colorado, the House of Representatives passed a resolution that all restrooms in the State House must be redesigned so they are sex-integrated.
>
> In Spring Grove State Hospital, Spring Grove, Maryland, fifty men and women share a large dormitory that includes a bedroom, sitting room, and a common bathroom (which has no partitions between the toilets or bathroom proper).
>
> In Lancaster, Pennsylvania, a judge handed down a verdict that it was okay for women to swim nude with men at the YMCA.
>
> In Chattanooga, Tennessee, a judge ordered a woman awaiting trial on civil cases to be put in a cell with a man. The

result was that the judge gave the man a three-month sentence for attempted rape.

In Hellerton, Pennsylvania, a woman who weighed only 120 pounds was ordered by her employer to lift boxes of spark plugs weighing 90 pounds each. She could not comply and lost her job and unemployment compensation.

In Berwick, Pennsylvania, women were compelled to work twelve hours a day without a lunch hour. They were told by their employers that they could only leave their stations in an emergency.

In Pennsylvania, all sports are sex-integrated. The physical-education classes are now sex-integrated ... where boys who formerly played basketball, football, and so forth, they are now having dancing, instead.

ERA enthusiasts persistently foster the misconception that the amendment will help women gain equal employment. The leaders of the feminist movement know better and are very reluctant to debate any knowledgeable person on that subject, fully aware that the Equal Employment Act of 1972 already assures women equal job opportunities. It is now illegal to discriminate in hiring because of sex. Because ERA advocates know that equal employment is the one strong card going for them, they continually misrepresent that to the American public.

The ERA is not popular with the public. Several surveys indicate that, if put to the test of a popular vote, it would fail utterly. Yet thirty-three leading magazines, all in the same month, orchestrated the passage of ERA. Why? Because the media, including some of the leading monthly and weekly magazines, are controlled by humanists.

President Carter has determinedly promised the feminist movement that he will push ERA through at least three more states, to assure ratification. What is his motivation? It certainly cannot be his approval of homosexuality and permissive lesbianism. However, it could be he fears losing the feminist vote.

TV: mind control. The most powerful vehicle in controlling the minds of a generation is television. Scientists tell us we remember 60 percent of what we see and only 10 percent of what we hear. Because TV and movies combine *both* primary entries to the mind—seeing and hearing—they became the principal targets of the humanists.

It is obvious, by the degenerate programming that has appeared in recent years, that the three major networks (ABC, NBC, and CBS) are predominantly controlled by amoral humanists. A medium that once featured family-oriented programming and observed discretionary moral standards now makes jokes about homosexuality, incest, wife swapping, and depravity. One network seems bent on being not only immoral in its programming, but anti-Christian.

As bad as TV "entertainment" (or debauchery) is, the news reporting is even more dangerous. More people get their current-events information today through TV news than from any other source. Most cities have a local affiliate station of one of the three major networks. Consequently, the news staff of the three networks control the slant of the news in a liberal, humanist direction. Not all the fifty or so people who control network news are committed humanists, but most of them are. If you doubt that, then I ask you to name one nationally known commentator who is a strong conservative. Humanists tend to be liberal in their world view, while pro-moralists tend to be conservative. (Naturally, there are exceptions on both sides.) Would not a free medium represent both liberal and conservative points of view? The following diagram portrays the five basic philosophies current in America:

SUPER LIBERAL	LIBERAL	MODERATE	CONSERVATIVE	SUPER CONSERVATIVE

Now, write in the name of your favorite national TV newsperson; then locate others you know. You will find a few moderates, several liberals, and a few superliberals. Did you find one conservative? Personally, I do not know *one*.

Many surveys of our populace's political preferences during the past decade show that the majority are conservative. Scores that I have seen range from 58 percent to 72 percent. The largest self-rating of "liberal" has been 32 percent, and several much less. At this juncture, we must ask: If the majority of our population considers itself conservative, but we do not have one single newsperson to offer a conservative perspective, are we really getting the news or a liberal slant to the news?

I did not appreciate this dilemma until the presidential election of 1964, which pitted the conservative Senator Barry Goldwater against the liberal Vice-President Lyndon Johnson. During that campaign, I watched Goldwater's position distorted dreadfully and consistently by the three networks. He was made to appear an unstable radical. In fact, that campaign contained the worst political advertisement I have ever seen on TV. Several times, a thirty-second commercial showed a little girl, picking a daisy in a field; then a hand, pushing the presidential hot button in the White House; followed by the girl being engulfed in a nuclear-bomb cloud. Following this appeared a radical-looking picture of Senator Goldwater and the question: "Do you want his hand on the button?" To my knowledge, there was not one cry of foul or dirty tricks or unfair advertising by television medium. It was consistent in its silence.

In spite of such distortions of his views and character, Senator Goldwater received 27 million votes. Since that election, not one single TV newsperson has represented the 27 million conservatives who showed their convictions by voting for the senator. Does that sound like a free and representative press to you?

Watch the commentaries after presidential debates or speeches. Hasn't it seemed strange to you that conservative spokesmen—those who favor traditional moral values and free enterprise—are held up to ridicule and criticism by the reviewers, as they subtly endorse or approve the liberal candidate's views? Clearly the television medium is used to promote those who hold to liberal, humanist positions.

Slanted presentations help to explain why a nation that calls itself conservative consistently votes a majority of liberals into public office. That would not happen if we had an objective medium. Nor would it occur if we had a fourth TV network, committed to rendering a conservative view of the news. The very mention of this, however, makes humanists paranoid in their use of such expressions as "mind control," "a threat to free speech," or "Gestapo tactics." Remember this about humanists: The only fairness doctrine they believe in is the right to present humanism as the only valid viewpoint. They know giving equal time to such things as profamily, prolife, pro-morality, and pro-American values would prove devastating to their objective of national—and ultimately world—control.

The 1976 presidential election provides another subtle illustration of humanist media bias. During the primaries, two former governors were candidates for the presidency. James E. Carter had governed the state of Georgia for four years, 1971–1974, where he had increased taxes, deficit spending, and size of the government. Ronald Reagan had been the governor of the largest state in the union for eight years, 1967–1974, where he reduced the size of government, welfare, and waste, leaving the state with over 500 million dollars in its treasury. In fact, if California's budget and gross state product were compared to other nations, California would be listed as the eighth largest country in the world. During the campaign, the news media referred to candidate Carter as Governor Carter; but when they mentioned Governor Reagan, it was usually as Mr. Reagan or Ronnie Reagan. Some call that reporting; I call it political bias.

These presidential-election illustrations are used because they are past history, verifiable, and probably within your memory. But the same devices are used in state and local elections today. This kind of media electioneering is not always successful, of course. Sometimes the media favorites are so superliberal that their radical, socialist views cannot be disguised, and thus they are defeated at the polls. But when an election is close, the media usually make the difference.

Nuclear energy provides another illustration of the liberal media's bias. One week before the Three Mile Island crisis, the *Today* show presented a special program warning against the dangers of nuclear energy. The day the mishap occurred, I counted eleven times in two hours that they showed film of the atomic plant and gave the warning of nuclear fallout and danger, in terms that would petrify anyone living in the state. In fact, the repetitious mention in all the media almost caused a dangerous panic condition. As it turned out, according to *U.S. News and World Report,* the radiation fallout from the Three Mile Island plant endangered no one and was equivalent to the radiation one would receive from six dental X rays.

I am not attempting to make a case for nuclear energy; that's out of my field. But my point is that the antinuclear bias of the media is apparent by the way they have covered the issue. If they really wanted to zero in on an issue related to saving the lives of Americans, why don't they organize a campaign of getting tough on the biggest killers in the country—drunk drivers? The following chart puts it in perspective for me:

Deaths During a Five-Year Period

235,000 . . . . by auto accidents
10,000 . . . . by farm machinery
2,000 . . . . by airline accidents
1,000 . . . . by bathtub accidents
150 . . . . by dam tragedies
0 . . . . by nuclear power plants

As almost any highway-patrol officer will confirm, an estimated 50 percent of all auto deaths are caused by drunk drivers. Except during the Christmas season, little mention is made by media humanists regarding the innocent victims of this national danger—yet we continually hear about the dangers of "nukes."

An even greater threat to our nation is that Russia will soon have nuclear superiority over America. During my last visit to Washington, I attended a briefing that announced military experts have documented this fact: In "1,000 days, Russia will surpass the United States in nuclear power and delivery capability." The report pointed out that, even if we launched a crash military-preparedness program, barring some unforeseen factor, it would be impossible to overtake the Russians. That is, even if we were to develop the B-1 bomber, produce multiple-warhead missiles, or complete other projects, the time lag between authorization and production is greater than 1,000 days!

Have you heard that on the news? Why isn't such a dangerous possibility newsworthy to our liberal or humanist newspeople? Because they have bought the idealistic concept of the humanists that Communism is not a threat to America. They say once we disarm, the Russians will become peaceloving.

That is partially true. They will become "piece loving"—a piece of California, a piece of New York, a piece of your state. With our media controlled by that kind of thinking, it is no wonder that a backward country like Russia, with an inferior economic system, is rapidly gaining supremacy over us.

TV talk shows. A good deal of mindless chatter is heard on TV talk shows, but to the discerning ear, an abundance of humanist propaganda is communicated, as well. The overwhelming number of guests or stars are predominantly amoral in their beliefs or immoral in their personal lives. Occasionally a Christian or conservative guest is invited, just to throw a sop to the fairness doctrine, but I would judge this is only one out of thirty—in a population in which one out of five professes Christianity outright and a large majority believe in a society based on the moral principles of the Ten Commandments.

Admittedly, much that appears on these shows is not filled with ideological propaganda. On the other hand, some of it is. Spokeswomen asked to represent the American homemaker have commented, for instance, that "Homemaking is a bore." Why do they ask that of the humanist representative of a feminist organization? How would she know? She never married or had children. But that is not pointed out on the show, because it might spoil her chance to promote her cause on national TV. I have seen so-called sexologists (humanist experts on sex and marriage) offer very bad—and, in some cases, harmful—advice on such subjects, abetted by the talk-show host, who speaks admiringly and respectfully to this so-called expert.

By contrast, have you noticed that the person who holds a pro-moral position is often attacked or ridiculed? The guest is almost treated as a threat to the personal life-style or beliefs of the host. I have no objection to such humanist ideology being communicated on TV, for we can always shut it off, if we choose. But I must ask: Why is there no network that rejects all

programming that is amoral and majors in wholesome entertainment? Certainly not because there aren't enough people
who would prefer it to the degenerate fare that is common
today. The humanists see TV as a vehicle, first, to indoctrinate
and second, to make money. Shortly after learning that Norman Lear was the producer of six of the most amoral "com-
edy" series on TV (such as the infamous *Mary Hartman, Mary
Hartman*), I had lunch with a Christian businessman who told
me how relieved he was to have sold his cable TV stations.
Guess who bought them? Norman Lear. No wonder our Lord
said, "The children of this world are wiser than the children of
light" (*see* Luke 16:8).

If all this is hitting you for the first time, don't discard it as
preposterous. File it on the back burner of your brain and
begin to analyze how TV is used to promote liberal or antimoral books or causes that communicate humanist ideology,
while ignoring the other side. Very few Christian authors or
recording artists are interviewed on TV; in fact, it is so hard to
penetrate the humanist wall that several big publishers of
Christian books don't even try. We have good books and articulate, interesting authors, but we contradict their religious beliefs—or those of the shows' controllers. Christians may appear
on a handful of local shows, but except for Billy Graham or
Pat Boone, few others make it on the national scene.

TV can be a marvelous means of communication, depending
on who controls it. Fortunately, a courageous few—Jerry Falwell, the Radio Bible Class, Pat Robertson, Rex Humbard, and
others—use it to communicate their moral and Christian convictions. Without their voices, this valuable medium would be
overwhelmingly in the hands of humanists or those influenced
by them.

The movie industry. Volumes could be written, documenting
the devastating effect of Hollywood and its amoral entertain-

ment on America's morals in the past fifty years. They attempt to excuse their exaltation of infidelity, violence, and corruption by suggesting they are "Just supplying the public with what it wants." Nonsense! Some of the best-loved films and excellent money-makers—such as *The Sound of Music* or *Mary Poppins*—have been clean and family oriented.

For the most part, Hollywood fare shocks the sensibilities of pro-moral citizens. Just a month ago, a very successful wheat broker sat next to me on a plane going to Kansas City. He was not an active churchman but did want his three teenage children to be raised with moral values. As we talked about the depraved kind of movies coming out of Hollywood, he told of an incident that happened three weeks before. He had taken his family to a well-advertised film, only to be so disgusted with its moral filth that he made his family leave with him only ten minutes into the story.

Hollywood uses immoral or amoral stories and plays not because they make good art, but because they offer a tremendous vehicle for assaulting the minds of our citizens with their humanistic beliefs. Once you understand the doctrines of humanism, you will find them subtlely slipped into these stories— sometimes obtrusively.

There is one easy way to illustrate whose team Hollywood has really been on during the last fifty years. They rarely make a film that shows Communism as a world aggressor or murderer of people—particularly of their own. Anti-German and anti-Japanese films abound, and many disclose the seamy side of America, but when is the last time you saw an anti-Soviet film? It certainly isn't because KGB movies would not have intrigue or drama. Sixty years of Communist crime against humanity provide ample material to draw on, but not if you're afraid to show humanistic socialism in a bad light. That protective aspect of Hollywood isn't hard to understand, for many of us remember when ten leading screenwriters were sent to jail as Communists, back in the 1950s. We may not remember, however, that all but two of them were reemployed by Hollywood after serving time (the other two died). Many of the top humanists in the film industry never forgave the government for that invasion of their right to pollute the minds of our nation with their humanist religion. Is it any wonder that radical liberal causes are usually endorsed by the *Who's Who* of Hollywood? Now that John Wayne has passed away, it is hard to find a Hollywood personality who takes a strong stand on morals and America.

When you read a list of Hollywood notables endorsing the ERA, homosexuality, abortion, marijuana, disarmament, and everything else that is harmful to America, just remember that a humanist stands up for his humanistic beliefs. To be sure, he has that right in a free society, and we wouldn't want it any other way. One thing about humanist notables is they are not hesitant to be aggressive in standing for their faith, freely using their influence to modify our society. We Christians live our faith and are willing to die for it, but until recently, we have been afraid to stand up for it and let our voices be heard in opposing the amoral humanizing of our culture. Sometimes I am nauseated by the passive Christian leaders (and followers) who say, "I know you're right, but I just don't want to get involved." That attitude is totally unscriptural, and it explains why we are losing the *battle for the mind.*

The power of Hollywood to influence our society toward amoral humanism should not be underestimated. Almost every day, several Hollywood films are featured on national TV, giving their subtle "art forms" access to the minds of our citizens. It is no wonder that Hollywood's amoral standards of the 1960s and 1970s have become the norm for TV programming in the 1980s. After all, the TV and movie screenwriters, producers, actors, and so forth are the same people who have been corrupting the nation's morals for decades with their humanistic beliefs.

Fortunately, some Christians are beginning to get into the movie business and provide the public with an alternative, but it will be an uphill fight all the way—not because Christians and other pro-moral Americans lack talent, but because for the most part, humanists control the outlets. I predict that the next few years will feature an increase in wholesome, profamily entertainment, but it will come *in spite of* the usual Hollywood channels, not through them.

The city of Dallas is the only city at present that has its own movie-review committee: the Dallas Motion Picture Classification Board. Twenty-six unpaid people were appointed to rate films with minors in view, taking advantage of a 1968 United States Supreme Court ruling that upheld the right of communities to limit young people's exposure to books and films that cannot be denied to adults. The board members discovered that Hollywood's so-called rating system (which is like asking Adolf Hitler to make a judgment on the justice of killing millions of Jews) was inadequate. As could be expected, cries of censorship flowed from Hollywood, which insisted that the twenty-six were not qualified to judge films. It didn't occur to Hollywood's filmmakers that their products prove *them* to be unqualified in determining what is moral and what is degrading. One Dallas board member's response was interesting: "We may not be qualified to rate movies, but we're qualified to tell what we would like our children to see."[125]

Hollywood will never improve its movie morals unless forced by community pressure to do so. If every pastor and pro-moral parent in the country would write his city mayor and councilman, we could force a degree of moral sanity on Hollywood. That kind of moral activism has been sadly lacking in America.

A Myriad of Humanist Organizations By this time, you are probably wondering why Christians were sound asleep back in the 1920s, when movies and radio got their start, but humanists were ready to move into these fields. Obviously, they saw the arts and the theater as excellent vehicles to communicate to the mind. That is why Voltaire, Rousseau, and Machiavelli wrote plays. Mixing their religious doctrine into art, they created the only vehicles open to humanists, who were in the minority and were opposed by the government and clergy during their lifetime. For instance, watch George Bernard Shaw's 1905 classic, *Arms and the Man,* and extract its anti-Czarist message to the people—published just twelve years before the Bolshevik Revolution.

Nineteenth-century Christians either disapproved of the arts or didn't recognize their power as vehicles of communication. Consequently, they were light years behind the humanists when radio and movies became available after the turn of the century. When TV came into prominence, the humanists were ready to move ahead once again. It pains me to remember that the son of the owner of several southern California radio stations told me fifteen years ago that I should apply for a "UHF TV license for only ten thousand dollars. Someday they will be worth a fortune." Unfortunately, I was sound asleep. Now I realize what a powerful tool I would have had to communicate the Gospel, morality, family living, and good, old-fashioned American patriotism. Oh, well, we live and learn!

Please understand: All those who pioneered the entertainment industry were not humanists. Some were patriotic, some saw it as a means of making money, and others aspired to fame or power. But the humanists saw it as a tool. If they couldn't buy a studio or station, they would work in the industry. I have no doubt the high priests of humanism taught their young disciples that the entertainment fields were to be prominent on their vocational priority list—along with journalism, school-teaching, law, government, publishing, the arts, and even the liberal clergy of both Protestant and Catholic churches. If that was their practice in the first part of the twentieth century, it is no wonder they have gained a virtual stranglehold on most of those fields today.

Cultural and ethical societies. The American Ethical Union, founded in 1889 in New York City, was a federation of over thirty ethical societies that had been initiated by Felix Adler more than a decade earlier. New York became the capital of the humanist movement, which then spread across the United States. The recognized liberalization of the East Coast can be traced largely to these early humanist organizations and the concentration of educational institutions located there. No doubt the rapid expansion of such societies to positions of influence was due to the many colleges and universities in the area.

The humanists soon found that establishing a myriad of organizations and societies would give them access to many more special-interest groups throughout the nation. One of the early organizations was the National Association for the Advancement of Colored People (founded in 1909–1910), followed by the Chicago Urban League (1917), both formed by ethical societies. Today, Chambers states, in almost every city where there is an ethical society, its members work closely with the Urban League.[126]

Since then, scores of organizations have been spawned or assisted by these societies, such as Americans for Democratic Action (ADA); the American Ethical Union (AEU); the American Civil Liberties Union (ACLU); and, more recently, the Sex Information and Education Council of the United States (SIECUS) and National Organization of Women (NOW). Many of these organizations show an interlocking of the same founders who, along with their disciples, were the

originators and directors of UNESCO, UNICEF, and the
United Nations World Health Organization.

These many humanist organizations supplied the humanists
with the ideal springboard from which to vault into government, both as elected politicians and as career diplomats and
government bureaucrats. Consequently, they were ready and
experienced in 1945, when the UN was formed, and they have
used the UN and its above-mentioned organizations to influence the world toward humanist goals. By getting their leaders
appointed to UN commissions, which was easily arranged
through their humanist influences in Washington, they have
used the vast fortune paid by the United States for support of
the UN to advance the cause of world humanism. (For a detailed study of these interlocking efforts, see Claire Chambers's
500-page, well-documented book *The SIECUS Circle*.)

The American Civil Liberties Union. The most effective humanist organization for destroying the laws, morals, and traditional rights of Americans has been the ACLU. Founded in
1920, it is the legal arm of the humanist movement, established
and bolstered by the Ethical Culture Movement. The anti-
Christian, anti-American, and pro-socialist causes espoused by
the ACLU should not be surprising, when one identifies its
founders and understands their philosophy. Its first chairman
was Dr. Harry Ward, professor of social ethics at Union Theological Seminary, a man who for thirty years worked tirelessly
to socialize the United Methodist Church. The well-known
parallel between the social positions of the Methodist Church
and the Communist Party can be attributed largely to Dr.
Ward's thirty years of indoctrinating the young, impressionable minds of Methodism's finest ministerial candidates.

Other influential ACLU founders were William Z. Foster,
formerly the head of the United States Communist Party; Dr.
John C. Bennett, a president of Union Theological Seminary;

humanists John Dewey, Clarence Darrow, Norman Thomas, Roger Baldwin; and many others, including Corliss Lamont. After ten years under the directorship of Roger Baldwin, the ACLU was probed by the United States House of Representatives special committee to investigate Communist activities in the United States. On January 17, 1931, the committee report stated:

> The American Civil Liberties Union is closely affiliated with the Communist movement in the United States, and fully 90 percent of its efforts are on behalf of communists who have come into conflict with the law. It claims to stand for free speech, free press, and free assembly; but it is quite apparent that the main function of the A.C.L.U. is to attempt to protect the communists in their advocacy of force and violence to overthrow the Government, replacing the American flag by a red flag and erecting a Soviet Government in place of the republican form of government guaranteed to each State by the Federal Constitution.[127]

According to the California state legislative committee that investigated un-American activities in 1943 and 1948, "The American Civil Liberties Union may be definitely classed as a Communist front or 'transmission belt' organization." A police undercover agent, David E. Gumaer, revealed in 1969 that "206 past leading members of ACLU had a combined record of 1,754 officially cited Communist front affiliations." He continued: "The present ACLU Board [as of 1969] consists of sixty-eight members, thirty-one of whom have succeeded in amassing a total of at least 355 Communist Front affiliations. That total does not include the citations of these individuals which appear in reports from the Senate Internal Security Subcommittee."[128]

Other activities of the ACLU will sound familiar to anyone conversant with the historical events of the past two decades:

- Legal defense for those who have supported Fidel Castro
- Legal defense for the Communist DuBois Clubs
- Dogged opposition to voluntary prayer and Bible reading in the public schools
- Antagonism toward laws which control subversive organizations
- Efforts to subtract the words "under God" from our Pledge of Allegiance
- Opposition to the repeal of state narcotics laws

Leaving no stone unturned in its effort to weaken and undermine the American way of life, ACLU had managed to capture control of the 1968 Presidential Commission on Obscenity and Pornography through its chairman, William Lockhart, and its general counsel, Paul Bender, both of whom were ACLU members. It was no surprise that, in 1970, the ACLU-dominated Commission issued a call for a federally financed " 'massive sex education effort' among adults and youths involving the family, school, church, and other agencies," as a means of combating pornography. Ably promoting this neatly packaged conclusion with personally prepared testimony before the Commission was none other than SIECUS executive director Mary Calderone.[129]

The ACLU, with its many chapters all over the country, has worked tirelessly against all laws forbidding pornography. Then certain leaders got themselves appointed to a presidential commission that called for federally funded sex education (which now floods the schools with amoral, humanistic, SIECUS materials, which recommend the erotic and sometimes pornographic *Sexology* magazine). Score: Humanism— 7, Christianity and moral sanity—0.

The anti-Christian attitude of the ACLU is not only evident in its persistent attack on moral legislation but also in its efforts to compel our country to become totally secular. We heard their outcries when "In God We Trust" was stamped on our coins and "under God" was added to the Pledge of Allegiance.

Every Christmas, they do battle with the religious symbols that remind people of the virgin-born Son of God. Two weeks before Christmas, 1979, an Associated Press report stated that the ACLU had received a favorable ruling on a lawsuit ordering the nativity scene removed from the Denver, Colorado, city-owned buildings, claiming that "the religious theme violated the separation of church and state." When the city appealed the ruling, it was overturned, but the ACLU had made its point. They will continue to harass our society until we are as humanistic as they; and don't think for a moment they won't be successful, unless we vigorously oppose them.

Their successes in our public schools are well documented. Because of them, prayer, Bible reading, Bible study, released-time classes, Easter, and Christmas celebrations have been eliminated. Easter has been changed to "spring break," Christmas to "winter vacation." Christmas programs can feature Santa, Rudolph, and Scrooge—but not the One whose entrance into the world we are celebrating.

For over twenty years, I have watched ACLU lawyers readily come to the aid (and often for minimal or no legal fees) of anyone who has a conflict with morality, human rights, civil disobedience, or anything else that further chips away the foundation stones of biblical morality upon which this country was founded. Frequently I have asked: Where are the Christian attorneys who tire of ACLU lawyers getting the courts so fouled up that, by the time a police officer finishes the paperwork on a thief or murderer, he is out on the street? Where were they when the courts were prevailed on by humanist attorneys to put prayer and Bible reading out of our formerly God-conscious public schools? Only in recent years have Christian attorneys banded together to form Christian legal-defense leagues or defend Christian schools.

Humanist attorneys, from Clarence Darrow to William Kuntsler (cited by the House Internal Security Committee in

1970 as "Communist oriented" according to Chambers), have so cleverly manipulated attacks on our time-honored institutions and basic moral practices that criminals are barely slapped on the wrist for invading the rights of law-abiding citizens. It will take an equal number of dedicated Christian attorneys to defend our culture from further erosion of its moral foundations and return our nation to moral sanity.

The American Humanist Association. According to Chambers, the AHA was established in Illinois as a ...

> non-profit, tax-exempt organization conceived for educational *and religious* purposes. With the signing of the incorporation papers, this group became the formal representative of Humanists in the United States and Canada. Although AHA "stemmed largely from Unitarianism as a movement of Religious Humanists," other originators included Universalists, Ethical Society leaders, professors of philosophy and education, scientists, heads of smaller Humanist factions, rationalists, and other freethinkers.
>
> So far as its physical structure is concerned, the AHA is the command vessel for a flotilla of federated associations that are moored in strategic locations in the United States and Canada. Humanist House, the AHA's official headquarters in San Francisco, is a five-story mansion overlooking Golden Gate Bridge and the Pacific Ocean. This building was officially opened on December 10, 1967, Human Rights Day, with the raising of the United Nations flag.[130]
>
> Like its affiliates, AHA directs its energies toward a seemingly endless list of "religious," educational, social, cultural, and scientific interests. In the fall of 1973, AHA leaders and their Humanist associates updated the first *Humanist Manifesto,* for the purpose of making clear which interests warrant top priority as Humanists approach the twenty-first century. Like the original Manifesto, *Humanist Manifesto II* criticizes religious dogmatism and denies the existence of a Creator. It

asserts that humans alone must solve the problems that threaten their existence on earth, stating: "No deity will save us; we must save ourselves." As its answer to mankind's present plight, the document affirms, among other things, the right to complete sexual freedom, birth control, abortion, divorce, euthanasia, and suicide.[131]

The Humanist is the bimonthly official magazine of the humanist movement in America. As such, it is readily available to college students in their library (at taxpayers' expense). This magazine provides leading humanists an opportunity to express their humanistic views to one another, and they speak out on most current topics.

In 1963 a group of liberal Humanist clergymen founded the FRH [Fellowship of Religious Humanists] with the aim of drawing into the Humanist movement Protestant ministers who regard Humanism as a religion. Located in Yellow Springs, Ohio, this Humanist faction is affiliated with the American Ethical Union, the American Humanist Association, the Unitarian-Universalist Association, and the International Humanist and Ethical Union.[132] FRH publishes a quarterly journal, *Religious Humanism,* and a membership bulletin, *The Communicator,* in addition to sponsoring conferences with the above groups and another less-well-known fraternal organization, the Society for Humanistic Judaism.[133] A branch of FRH's Humanist Center Library is located at Cocoa Beach, Florida. This library houses the archives of the humanist movement in America. FRH stands among those who voice the hope that a "comprehensive world religion will develop through the creative processes of our times."[134]

The influence of these organizations on government is easily illustrated for the astute observer. For example, during the Iranian crisis of late 1979 and early 1980, three liberal ministers were permitted to go to Tehran, to conduct religious services for the hostages confined at the United States embassy.

Even CBS news acknowledged the liberal and, in two cases, radical activist background of those clergymen. I would ask: Since there are probably 100 Bible-believing ministers in America with more influence and larger congregations, representing far more people, why wasn't one of them in the group? Even CBS did not know the basis of their selection.

Humanists use every opportunity to promote their causes and people, to make it appear they represent the majority of the American people. That is a farce. The National Council of Churches may have at one time represented the majority of Protestants in this country, but in the past thirty years its membership has gone down drastically, as the number of Bible-believing Christians has gone up. Why, then, this disproportionate public notoriety? Quite simply, it is because of humanist infiltration into government agencies and liberal religions. Whenever the government wants to hear from the religious community, it turns to the NCC, which only represents the minority but is more compatible with government's humanistic views.

Have you ever noticed that government diplomats often quote the World Health Organization on such issues as population control, birth control, abortion, and so forth? In so doing, they invariably publish scare statistics and make pronouncements that are antimoral. That should not be surprising, for many of the founders and leaders of the World Health Organization were signers of the *Humanist Manifesto,* which blatantly advocates the right to sexual freedom, abortion, birth control, divorce, euthanasia, and "death with dignity" (what we used to call suicide).

Dr. Francis Schaeffer and Dr. C. Everett Koop have warned our nation, in their book *Whatever Happened to the Human Race?,* their seminars, and their movies, to beware of the euthanasia movement—that is, the killing of the elderly. When it becomes more prominent, look for a "scientific" endorsement from the prestigious World Health Organization. Remember, humanists believe that the major decisions of the world should be made by the elite—and *they* are the elite.

The Vehicle of Government Never underestimate the importance of government. God didn't. He knew it would be the most harmful single organization ever conceived, if it fell into the wrong hands. For centuries, He kept Israel from choosing a king, but when the nation insisted upon a king, He granted its wish. Hebrew history shows that monarchy was either good or bad, depending on the moral convictions of the king. As Scripture warned, when the righteous bear rule, the people rejoice. Sin is a curse to any people (*see* Proverbs 29:2).

The power of government to influence and control the minds of a nation was certainly not lost on the humanists. While using their many organizations and the media to best advantage, they saw early the need of getting their humanist-minded people into office or identifying those already in office who were vulnerable to pressure.

Most Americans are confused about the political process, and relatively few realize its importance. The fear of being rejected keeps many good citizens from making an attempt to run for office. Additionally, Christians know that the media often attacks those with moral values and makes things difficult for their families. We need to remember that name recognition is the name of the game. That is: Run a person for an office such as school-board member, then move up to city or county council, then on to state or national office. A few well-known individuals have started with national office and made it, but most are obliged to run for office, lose an election but gain increased recognition, and repeat their attempt later. It is almost forgotten that President Abraham Lincoln was defeated twice before being elected congressman from Illinois.

Unlike the average Christian, who runs once and gives up if defeated, the humanists persist until they succeed. One southern California, eighteen-year, superliberal congressman was defeated three times before his humanist backers got him into office. But they consider their efforts well rewarded, for he has backed every humanist cause in the Congress since being elected.

The federal government consists of 537 elected officials— 435 representatives, 100 senators, a president, and a vice-president. Based on the decisions of these men and the amoral direction our country has gone during the past 30–40 years, there can be no question that the humanists control our government, and have for many years. That does not mean that all government officials are humanists. But those 537 people who control our national destiny represent sufficient humanistic philosophy or lack of true Christian consensus to have brought us to the threshhold of fulfilling the humanist dreams of a secular, amoral society. To understand this, let's examine the motivations of politicians.

The motivations of politicians. In our country, any citizen can be elected president of the United States or governor of his state or hold any of the thousands of offices in our land. All kinds of people become politicians. Some are very fine people, some represent harmful philosophies of life, and some are downright evil. Most people naively think that somehow people elected to public office get better with authority, whereas just the opposite is generally the case. An old political truism becomes obvious to anyone paying attention today: "Power corrupts, and absolute power corrupts absolutely!" Stalin's character did not improve when he became absolute dictator of Russia, as the tragic death toll in his country testifies. John Kennedy's morals did not improve when he moved to the White House, as subsequent stories reveal, and obviously President Nixon's true character was likewise not enriched.

A politician's decisions and actions, like those of any other human being, are going to flow naturally from his mental convictions. If he is a humanist, opportunist, pro-moralist, or committed Christian, he is going to act accordingly.

Generally speaking, you will find that politicians fall into one of the following five categories. Some, of course, waiver between two, depending on the issue.

COMMITTED HUMANISTS The voting record of a number of leading politicians at all levels shows them to be amoral humanists with strong socialistic convictions who, in the name of human rights, have deprived the country's pro-moral majority of the protection necessary to maintain a morally sane society. These are the legislators, judges, governors, attorneys-general, and so forth who have created the laws that enable porno publishers to pollute the minds of our young. They argue: "This is a free country, and we have the constitutional guarantee of freedom of the press. Therefore, anything a citizen wants to publish, he should have the right to publish." That parents should have the right to protect their children from the mental corruption of porno filth is not considered.

This demand for rights in the name of human dignity always comes at the expense of someone else's rights. For example, the same humanists demand that expectant mothers should have the right to choose an abortion. What about the unborn's right to life? Humanists have established themselves in positions where they become the gods who determine whose rights take precedence. That is why they are vigorously pushing the right of homosexuals to teach school, even though this is contrary to the rights of 95 percent of the country's parents, who want their children taught by heterosexuals. The fact that homosexuality is a learned behavior and that children with no predisposition toward it can be led into it by a homosexual teacher, particularly before puberty, is not even considered by humanists (*see* the author's book *The Unhappy Gays*). They are demanding homosexual rights in everything: housing, employment, marriage, and even adoption of children. In other words, an employer has no right to employ only heterosexuals, or a landlord has no right to rent only to heterosexuals. Humanists demand complete rights for those who choose the homosexual life-style.

If they succeed, through legislation, in forcing the pro-moral majority to accept homosexuality as normal behavior, contrary to biblical teaching, 3,000 years of Western culture, and over 300 years of American history, they will go on to other human rights—such as legalizing prostitution, drugs, gambling, and who knows what else? The demand of the humanists for complete human rights is not just a campaign; it is an *obsession.* Such individuals, in spite of political rhetoric, party, or lip service to religion, are unfit to hold office in this country. The sooner the millions of pro-moral voters realize this and rise up, replacing them with those who hold strong moral convictions, the better off this country will be.

Since politicians and educators draw their pay from taxpayers, they should represent them. I am convinced that modern humanists do not represent the majority of Americans. Until enough taxpayers realize they are being misrepresented by these "public servants," we will continue to see a minority of committed humanists lead our

CORRUPT POLITICIANS

country to the brink of moral destruction— particularly our young and future generations.

Some politicians, and only God knows how many, are evil men. They sell their Faustian souls to the industrialists or big corporations who get them elected. Consequently they vote whatever is in the best interests of their bosses. Some, particularly in city and state government, are financed by criminal figures, gamblers, or special-interest groups. Such individuals can hardly be expected to legislate pro-moral measures. While they are not really humanists, they share the humanist's amoral code of ethics, and they are sometimes even worse in their personal lives.

Usually these people vote along with the humanists on moral issues, but for different reasons. Their first consideration in voting is to please those who got them elected. Second, on issues that do not concern their bosses, they use their votes to insure debts on future voting issues that directly concern their bosses. (The average citizen has no idea how much trading of votes goes on behind legislative doors at all levels of government.) Morality and the country's best interest have a very low priority with such public officials. That is why voters should closely evaluate a politician's moral position and voting record. If he does not maintain a minimum standard of morality, he should be replaced by someone who will.

The mayor of a western city told me recently, "I have wanted to be a politician ever since I was a little boy." Many political leaders today could

PROFESSIONAL POLITICIANS

say the same thing. The field of government, especially the power and prestige it offers, are strong inducements to many individuals. And that is not all bad; we must have government officials, in order to maintain a sane, protected society. But the motivation of a person going into politics and his moral principles when he gets there will determine whether he protects the moral principles upon which this country was founded or whether his humanist colleagues can lead him into turning America into a virtual Rome or Pompeii.

Personal charisma and years in office are scarcely sufficient criteria for electing people to office, though in this day of TV exposure, that seems to win elections. Our citizens should be advised to test a candidate's moral convictions by looking at his voting record. Remember, a person's actions reflect his morals; that is nowhere more pronounced than in the political arena.

A state senator shared with me his analysis of politicians: "There are two things uppermost in the mind of a politician—getting elected and staying elected!" If that is true, and most knowledgeable people agree that it is, then we, as pro-moral Christians, need to put more pressure on these people, to help strengthen their convictions. When the moral majority that is finally awakening from its political apathy begins to drop thousands of letters on legislators' desks, and when we have replaced a few of their amoral colleagues, these professional politicians will get the message that Americans want to move back in the direction of morality. If they do not begin to lead us that way, they should be replaced.

In 1978, *Parade* magazine pointed out that the United States Senate contained seventeen millionaires. To some men and women who have made it in the business world or inherited a fortune, the political arena has more appeal than the tennis court or golf course. They have the money to finance an advertising campaign that the ordinary citizen could not begin to match. One man spent over $2 million of his own money to win an election.

POLITICAL OPPORTUNISTS

In addition to the rich, some well-known athletes, an astronaut, and others with widespread name recognition have run for office, some successfully. Senator John Glenn and the former quarterback for the San Diego Chargers and Buffalo Bills, New York representative Jack Kemp, are but two examples.

Americans (and probably all people) tend to be hero-worshipers, and since our heroes seem larger than life, we decide they must be inherently good. We need to view them realistically and critically. Some strong moralists have taken advantage of their political opportunity, and it shows in their voting record. Others, however, have failed the minimum morals test and should be replaced. How can you tell which they are? Their voting records are the acid test.

America has long enjoyed the dedicated service of strongly moral political leaders. Some have been outstanding Christians; others represent what Dr. Francis Schaeffer calls the Christian consensus (the biblical morality upon which this country was founded). Such pro-moral political leaders may be Protestants, Catholics, Mormons, or Jews. Though differing in theology, they are in harmony on such issues as abortion, homosexuality, pornography, prostitution, murder, integrity, and the responsibility of government to protect the family, not destroy it.

PRO-MORAL POLITICIANS

Unfortunately, the ranks of the pro-moralists have been shrinking during the past fifty years, until they are now in the minority. Such leaders need to be returned to office and joined by others who share their moral persuasion. Only then will we halt the tragic breakdown that finds us murdering, by abortion, more babies every four years than Adolf Hitler killed in World War II. The free use of drugs and pornography that is so harmful to our young will also be eliminated. These problems did not arise overnight and will not be cured quickly. But the first step toward their removal will be the elimination of amoral politicians from all levels of government and their replacement by those political leaders who share the convictions of the moral majority.

The political spectrum. More important than his political party is a government leader's position on the above political spectrum. Currently the pro-moralists—those who can always

COMMITTED HUMANISTS	CORRUPT POLITICIANS	PROFESSIONAL POLITICIANS	POLITICAL OPPORTUNISTS	PRO-MORAL POLITICIANS

be counted on to vote in favor of decency and family protection—number approximately 25 percent (using the voting record of Congress as an example). Another 10–15 percent of the professional politicians and political opportunists vote all or some of the time with the pro-moralists. The humanists and corrupt politicians can usually be counted on to vote the amoral cause.

By replacing the two groups on the left and some of those in the middle during the next few years, we could return moral sanity to the United States Senate, the House of Representatives, and ultimately to America. We do not need to replace all of the Congress. An additional 15 percent of pro-moralists would suffice, because with a solid group of 40 percent who would always vote for morality and the family, many of the middle-of-the roaders would swing to the moral position, providing a majority. In fact, two elections could dramatically change the climate of national government.

Conclusion

We have covered quite a bit of territory in pointing out the four vehicles used by the humanists to gain control of our nation: education, the media, organizations, and government itself.

At first glance it seems hopeless, for they seem to have all the resources. Don't you believe it! We have far greater assets. God is on our side, and we can identify thousands of faithful churches throughout our land. The Christian school movement is growing; there are millions of us—and only a handful of them. According to the August 26, 1973, issue of *The New York Times*, there were only about 250,000 humanists in America. Allowing for a 10 percent increase, they would number about 275,000 today. However, they occupy key positions of leadership, where they exercise an inordinate influence on America. With God's help and the active participation of the millions of pro-moral citizens in our land, we can legally remove these people from office and replace them with those who hold moral convictions.

9

The Moral Majority

With almost virtual control of the national media, newspapers, magazines, book distribution, education, and to a large degree, government, the humanists give the impression that

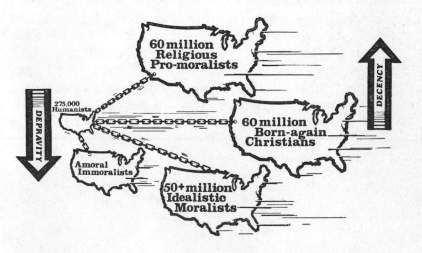

they speak for the majority in America. In reality, just the opposite is true. We have already noted that humanism only numbers about 275,000 members. If we grant that for every hard-core, doctrinaire humanist in America, there are 50 who have been seriously influenced to humanist-style thinking, they would still total less than 14 million. In a land of 220 million people, even that inflated figure is just over 6 percent of the population. Interestingly enough, a very scientific poll taken in 1979 showed that such a percentage represents the number of people in this country who do not believe in God, for the pollsters discovered that 94 percent of all Americans are theistic in their beliefs. Only 4 percent of our people explicitly deny the existence of a Supreme Being. (If a survey were made of atheists in this country, it is probable that a large percentage of them are employed in education, where they have access to the minds of our young.)

George Gallup, one of the most respected leaders in the scientific art of surveying a population, surprised the country in 1976 by announcing, "There are 50 million Americans who claim to have had a born-again experience." His organization's latest study, requested by *Christianity Today,* increased that figure, when it found that "better than one-third of the adult population have had a life-changing religious experience" (60 million of which identified that experience with Jesus Christ).[135] Since the survey indicated that young people are becoming evangelical Christians at a higher rate than did their parents, we can assume that 79 million out of our 220-million population would represent those who could loosely be called evangelical.

The True Moral Majority

By analyzing Gallup's statistics, one can demonstrate that the overwhelming majority of Americans prefer a moral culture in which to raise their children. It is reasonable to assume that 50 million born-again adults in this country would vote for morality, in contrast to humanism's amorality, if the issues were made clear. We can add an equal number of pro-moral religious people from other churches, who would also vote the

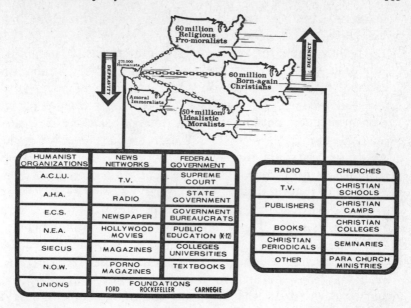

pro-moral cause if they saw it clearly. This 50 million would include Protestants who do not stress a born-again experience, Jews, Catholics, Mormons, and many others whose moral ideals are biblical. Interestingly enough, this totals the same number of adults Gallup discovered were church members— 100 million, or almost two-thirds of our adult population. (The reason for the apparent confusion in differing totals is because Gallup requested responses from only adults. I have tried to make conservative comparisons to the total population, because millions of young people and children are Christians.)

The other one-third of our population, although they do not attend church, are certainly not amoral. I would estimate that 30–50 million of them could be safely classified as idealistic moralists. That is, they were raised in a Christian consensus and possess a God-given, intuitive moral conscience. They may not live up to their moral ideals all the time, but they hold these values in high regard for the culture in which they live and raise their families.

The last group, the amoralists (or immoralists), is harder to pinpoint. As we have seen, at best, humanist thinkers can only account for about 14 million adults (and that is being very generous). Add to that the moral degenerates, such as gangsters, prostitutes, porno publishers, dope peddlers, some homosexuals, and others without any moral values, and we could add 5 to 10 million adults. Actually, no one knows for sure Using Gallup's discovery that 16 percent of our population does not believe that the Ten Commandments are for today, which would include amoral humanists, immoral degenerates, and others, we would still only estimate a total of 23 million people.

The obvious conclusion to all of this is that America is not a godless nation of hedonists without moral values. Yet we suffer from that reputation around the world, and we even admit to it ourselves. Actually, the humanist-controlled book industry, television industry, news networks, many humanist government officials, and Hollywood create that image and reputation, which is strongly out of proportion to the way we really are. Consider these other interesting statistics from the Gallup poll, based only on the adult population, age 18 and over (155 million):

69	million adults	hope to "go to heaven only because of their faith in Jesus Christ"
124	million adults	believe Jesus Christ is divine
65	million adults	believe the Bible is inerrant
77	million adults	believe that God created Adam and Eve
100	million adults	are members of churches or synagogues
40	million adults	attend church weekly
17	million adults	attend more than once a week
147	million adults	believe in God or a universal Spirit

140 million adults believe in life after death
132 million adults (84 percent) believe that the Ten Commandments are valid today

The above does not sound like a survey taken in a godless, humanistic society that is eagerly pursuing an amoral culture. Yet that is exactly what we are becoming. Those who have watched the practical morals of America are alarmed at the increase in promiscuity, infidelity, divorce, homosexuality, and abortion—all true signs of a decaying society. The leading question demands a serious answer: Are we decaying by natural processes, or by design?

Christianity Up—Morals Down

During the thirty years I have been a pastor, I have watched Christianity double in our country. After my discharge from the Air Force, I found only a handful of Christian colleges to choose from. Today there are scores of good Bible-believing colleges for our youth. In addition, all the old ones have at least doubled in size. While liberal seminaries, totally infiltrated by humanism, have died or have been forced to merge with others, just to stay open, fundamental seminaries and Bible institutes have flourished, and new ones have started.

Thirty years ago, I only knew of two large churches—over 1,000 in attendance. Today there are over 100 such churches, with some "superchurches" running over 15,000 in membership. But it isn't just churches that have grown. Over 110,000 Bible-believing churches are spread throughout the country. One denomination I know (the Baptist Bible Fellowship) started from zero 28 years ago. Today it numbers over 2,500 churches, some of which are among the ten largest in the nation. In addition, millions of people attend "the electric church" of TV every Sunday. This was unknown, 30 years ago. During these 30 years, one phenomenon has helped to slow the humanist juggernaut considerably: the growth in Christian publishing. The humanists have such a stranglehold on secular publishing and the means of distribution that Christians started their own publishing houses, magazines, and periodicals. Today, millions of Christian books are produced annually, offering a pleasant alternative to amoral humanism.

If we had sufficient space, we could detail the scores of parachurch ministries, the over 350 Christian radio stations, Christian broadcasters, and the cable and satellite TV that is reaching millions more in our country.

Without a doubt, Christianity is on the rise in America—Gallup confirms that—yet we are daily confronted by the fact that our nation's morals are deteriorating rapidly. The reason ought to be clear, by this time. While we have been busy building our churches, schools, and ministries, a small but dedicated cadre of humanists has infiltrated the most influential pathways to the minds of our people: education, the media, organizations, and government. We Christians have almost totally abandoned the second-most-important field for influencing people today—government. We are satisfactorily represented in the first through the activities of the church, but we have neglected the second at our nation's peril! The following chart, identifying the most important means of communicating to the minds of people in order to influence their culture, tells the story:

- The church   ... Predominantly controlled by pro-
                      moralists
- Government ⎫
- Education   ⎬ ... predominantly controlled by hu-
                      manists
- Media   ⎪
- Organizations ⎭

It is obvious from this chart that, were it not for the powerful influence of the church on our society, America would be a humanist nation today. This also explains why educators, ACLU lawyers, media spokesmen, and many government officials are so hostile to the church (except the liberal, humanist churches of the National Council of Churches, which they largely control). The humanist movement recognized long ago that moral-minded, Bible-believing churches were their mortal enemy—and they have opposed them vigorously.

Unfortunately, many Christians have been sound asleep on this issue. In fact, many Christian leaders have been so busy fighting among themselves over doctrinal or denominational differences that they still do not recognize the true enemy. Unless these leaders open their eyes to the fact that America is being overrun with the atheistic, amoral religion of humanism and mount a united attack based on morality, humanism is sure to triumph.

Doctrinal Purity Versus Moral Degeneracy

For thirty years, I have been a biblical fundamentalist with strong doctrinal convictions. Any pastor or church leader in San Diego, where I have ministered for twenty-four years, will testify that I will not compromise my doctrinal integrity for anyone—and I have the scars to prove it. There are many groups in Christianity with which I cannot work in projects of evangelism or in areas that involve theology. The battle against humanism, however, is not theological; it is moral. Humanists have totally rejected God, creation, morality, the fallen state of man, and the free-enterprise system. As such, they are the mortal enemy of all pro-moral Americans, and the most serious threat to our nation in its entire history. Unless both Christian and non-Christian lovers of virtue stand together as upright citizens, humanists will turn this great land into another Sodom and Gomorrah.

When I was assigned to a B-29 flight crew as a waist gunner, I didn't ask the other ten men whether they were Catholics, Jews, or Protestants. I merely wanted to know if they could fly the plane or shoot the 50-millimeter machine guns. Later I discovered that the other waist gunner was a Mormon, the turret gunner a Catholic, and the tail gunner a Southern Baptist. We could never have worked together on a religious project (in fact, we could barely talk about theology without heating up), but on one fundamental we were in 100 percent agreement: We were all Americans interested in preserving our country's freedom.

Today the battle is not physical, but essentially moral. Unless a sufficient number of pro-moral Americans acknowledge that and are willing to do battle on a basis of common moral conviction, I see no hope for freedom in the twenty-first century. If, however, pro-moral leaders of all religious persuasions are willing to stand together as fellow Americans concerned with preservation of the family and moral decency, we can still win this relentless battle for our minds and those of our children.

Salty Saints

For 2,000 years, the church in the Western world has served as the moral conscience of society. In recent years, many church leaders have been intimidated into a reluctance to speak out on moral issues. Most have addressed them within the walls of their churches, of course, as if that fulfilled their responsibility. However, therein lies the problem. We in the Bible-believing church have done a reasonably good job of letting our light shine, but that is only half of our Lord's command to His church:

> You are the salt of the earth; but if the salt loses its flavor, how shall it be seasoned? It is then good for nothing but to be thrown out and trampled under foot by men. You are the light of the world. A city that is set on a hill cannot be hidden. Nor do they light a lamp and put it under a basket, but on a lampstand, and it gives light to all who are in the house. Let your light so shine before men, that they may see your good works and glorify your Father who is in heaven.
>
> Matthew 5:13–16 NKJB-NT

Our present society is in a state of moral decay, not because the majority of Americans love degeneracy, but because the influence of humanism has been greater on our culture than the influence of the church. Admittedly, we can tell thousands of thrilling stories of individuals whose lives have been transformed by a personal experience of faith in Jesus Christ, for we have been faithfully letting our light shine. But the fact remains that we have not been the moral salt in our community that we should be. We have failed to give moral leadership to our society.

I am convinced that believing correctly, "walking in the Spirit," or even aggressively sharing our faith with others falls short of our full responsibility. God expects us also to be our brother's keeper, the watchmen on the wall, the moral salt of the earth. Remember, our Lord condemned the hypocrisy of the Pharisees. He drove the money changers out of the temple and spoke out openly against the sins of the people. The twentieth-century church and its leaders can do no less!

Approximately 50 million school-age children are at stake. They are growing up in a moral vacuum, misled by educators to think of themselves as amoral primates. It is no wonder that they fail to morally distinguish their right hand from their left.

God saved Nineveh from destruction after the spiritual and moral repentance of the government leaders and the nation's adults, preserving the 60,000 children who knew not their left hand from their right. I believe He will save America, if the church will aggressively lead the pro-moral majority to stop this toboggan slide to depravity and return our nation to moral sanity.

That kind of moral revival will only come if today's faithful ministers, or shepherds of the sheep, will provide the kind of assertive leadership that Charles Wesley and George Whitfield conferred upon colonists in the early eighteenth century, bringing about the Great Awakening. We need to become more active in recruiting godly men to run for public office, where their moral influence can be felt. It is commendable that Christians pray for those in authority over them; we are commanded to do that. It is equally praiseworthy that several groups endeavor to lead our existing politicians to Christ. We need that. But we must also recognize that governors and government leaders are called "God's ministers" three times in Romans 13:1–7. We are in a moral quagmire today because ministers have failed to recruit "ministers of God" from our congregation, to run for public office.

My godly pastor echoed the unwise advice of many Christians during the early 1940s, when he taught, "Politics is a dirty business. Rather than getting involved in politics, we Christians should stick to preaching the gospel and let the nice, civic-minded people run the country." As a result, for forty years the American Humanist Association, the Ethical Cultural Union, the American Civil Liberties Union, and other humanist groups have backed their humanist candidates in both parties, gaining the strongest representation in our government. The limited number of Christian laymen who did run for office disregarded the advice of their pastors and usually enjoyed no help whatsoever from the morally minded members of their congregation.

I am not condemning my minister colleagues in the slightest. I certainly know where they are coming from, for I was there, just five years ago. Until then I had never recruited anyone for public office. God had used my life and that of our church staff to recruit almost 300 young people to enter the ministry or prepare for the mission field, but I had never actively solicited candidates for political office. Then, in the providence of God, I was subjected to a painful educational experience, when the church attempted to get a zoning variance passed by the city council. After three years of effort, we lost, 6 to 2. For the first time, I realized that men and women largely hostile to the church controlled our city. Gradually that has changed. Christians, backed by fellow Christians throughout the city, have won elections, and others who value high morals for our community have replaced humanists or those influenced in their thinking by humanists. These pro-moral additions have helped to crack down on massage parlors and porno shops, and churches are now given a fair hearing for their growth needs.

Let me show you one simple method by which ministers could change the moral climate of our age in just one decade. If all 110,000 ministers in our country would ask God to use them to recruit just two members each year to run for public office, starting with school boards, city councils, and so forth, assuming elections every other year, that would total 550,000 candidates. With adequate support from their friends, church associates, and neighbors, at least 25 percent would be elected. Many would gain name recognition and proceed to state and national office, and eventually a majority of the 537 now misrepresenting us in Washington would be replaced by those who would truly represent the moral majority.

Personally, I believe this plan is so practical and feasible that

I am praying for and looking forward to the day that I can enter the voting booth and have the luxury of choosing between two Christian candidates for the same national office. One city in Indiana, in which we held a seminar, has already enjoyed that privilege on the local level. Two Christian attorneys, members of the same Baptist church, became outraged at the district attorney for failing to prosecute the porno peddlers of their community. With their pastor's approval, they ran in their respective parties' primary for DA and won. On Election Day, the community had a choice between a Democrat and a Republican, both of whom were committed to morality. Now that is true Christian citizenship in action!

After a seminar in Illinois, where I had spoken out on the need for churches to start Christian schools because of the dangers of humanist teaching in the public schools, the seminar chairman drove me to the airport. To my surprise, he announced, "We don't have that problem in our community. Four of our five school-board members are born-again Christians, and we refuse to hire humanists in our system or use harmful textbooks." He then related their agreement that no member could leave the board until he recruited another pro-moral Christian candidate to take his place. If all 16,000 school districts in America were run that way, we could break the stranglehold that the humanists now have on the minds of America's youth.

Let's Hear it for Morality

We moralists have been silent long enough! Except for a few sporadic voices, Christians have somehow been reluctant to voice their political concerns. Since you now realize that we really represent the majority in this country, you must raise your voice so all can hear—from your neighborhood to the state house and then to the White House. I am convinced that people are waiting for moral leadership.

After carefully analyzing the data taken from grass-roots America, in "the most comprehensive study we have ever done in the area of religion,"[136] George Gallup said, "Americans want a vocal church on spiritual, moral, and ethical matters. People of all faiths want churches and other religious organizations to speak out. However, there is a sharp divergence of opinion among members of various denominations and faiths when it comes to political and economic matters. This, of course, should not surprise us."[137]

The electrifying response of Americans, both Catholic and Protestant, to the Pope's visit to the United States in 1979 ought to communicate loudly to Christian leaders throughout the country. Wherever he went, crowds appeared in greater numbers than anticipated. Never in my lifetime has an international religious figure spoken out so aggresssively on the issues that involve morality. And the stronger he addressed those issues, the greater grew the crowds.

The moral majority will follow, but they must hear a call to moral activism from their spiritual shepherds. The editors of *Christianity Today* had this in view when they added an interesting comment to the George Gallup article:

> ... the all too obvious failure of liberalism has coincided with a hunger for basic morality and a revitalization of fundamental Christianity. This has created a day of unprecedented opportunity for evangelicals to present the gospel to the world in which we live as well as to effect substantive changes for good within our own society. We must now show the world that evangelicals care and know how to translate theology into compassionate action.[138]

I could not agree more! Our caring should be demonstrated in our: evangelism—showing our concern for the souls of men;

in brotherly love—showing that we care for them as people (when they hurt, we should be the first to help); in moral activism—showing that we love their children by voicing our opposition to amoral legislation and advocating morality on the part of government. This will also mean that we get involved in the electoral process as faithful citizens, either as candidates ourselves or as workers assisting the right kind of candidates. We must be more vocal in letting existing political leaders know our opinion on pending government actions that involve morals.

To be specific, Christians should raise their voices, from their homes, churches, and places of business, whenever matters come up regarding the following:

- *Abortion* We must also forbid the use of tax moneys for this form of child murder.
- *Homosexuality* Our laws are already too weak in this area. This will include opposition to ERA, for it opens the door to homosexuality.
- *Pornography* We need laws to eliminate all pornography from our land.
- *Prostitution* This is a blight to any society.
- *Gambling* It is wrong and breeds crime.
- *Infanticide and Euthanasia* Only God can exercise the right to decide who has the right to live.
- *Parents' Rights* God gave parents the right and responsibility to raise their children. Until government figures out a way to bear children, it must refrain from usurping parents' rights.
- *Drugs* Drugs destroy the body, impair the judgment, and twist the morals of a person. They should be opposed vigorously, unless prescribed by competent medical authorities for limited periods of time.
- *Religious Humanism* Any and all forms should be vigorously opposed, particularly in government and education.

If a sufficient number of Christians would speak out on the above issues, more than enough morally minded people in our land would act to stop our descent into amorality and return our nation to moral self-respect. Make sure you never vote for anyone who does not share the above minimum moral convictions, and encourage your friends to do the same.

10

The Sleeping Majority Is Stirring

A visible ground swell of renewal is taking place in our country, within both the Christian and the nonchurch, pro-moral segment of society. The moral chaos produced by seven decades of humanist teachings and the antimoral activism of the homosexuals, feminists, and other so-called human-rights advocates are becoming increasing sources of alarm to citizens from all walks of life.

Only an extreme radical looks with pleasure on the alarming divorce rate (over 1,125,000 divorces in 1979), increasing child abuse, the increase in crime, and other obvious signs of a decadent society. Our people are becoming concerned to the point of alarm. Gradually they are realizing that these social ills have increased in direct proportion to the growing control of our society by humanism.

The homosexual and media attacks on Anita Bryant and the good people of Dade County, Florida, forced many people to awaken to the seriousness of the situation. Some of our church leaders who foresaw the crisis two decades ago have been busy founding Christian schools, largely as a reaction to amoral humanism in public education. For many years, we safely committed our children to the public schools for a traditional, God-conscious (though not aggressively religious) education. In addition, we provided extensive Bible training in church,

Sunday school, youth meetings, released-time education, and vacation Bible schools. With the aggressive takeover of public education by the humanists, however, this approach has long since become obsolete, resulting in the amazing growth of Christian schools. In fact, the Christian-school movement is the fastest growing movement in America. At this present rate of growth (one new school every seven hours), and with the increasing violence and chaos in the public sector, it is expected that by 1990–1992, 51 percent or more of America's schoolchildren will be educated at their parents' expense in private schools, most of which are church related or sponsored. Obviously, parents are concerned!

For some church leaders, it took humanist-inspired attacks on the Christian schools of Ohio and the parents of the children in those schools to awaken them. For others, it took an unfriendly city hall, when they sought laws to stop nudity, pornography, and homosexuality. For others like myself, it took failure to get fair treatment from government officials when seeking church building permits. For some, it took humanist opposition to Lester Rolloff, for operating homes for wayward youth that were far more effective than state-run institutions. For some, it was the vicious attack on the Christian-school movement by the IRS, which demanded we prove our innocence in regard to racial discrimination, in order to keep from losing our nonprofit tax status. This reversed the time-honored protection of Americans under the law, which declares that a citizen is considered innocent unless proved guilty. Only a massive letter-writing campaign thwarted the IRS commissioner in his attempt to financially ruin the Christian-school movement and force our children back into humanist-dominated schools. Even then, it took the courageous efforts of Congressman Robert Dornan, Senator Jesse Helms, and others to forbid the IRS to pursue that approach. Unfortunately, that issue will come before Congress again, so unless we elect more pro-moralists to Washington posts, the IRS may ultimately prevail.

Many leaders of that successful letter-writing campaign were ministers. They had not missed the IRS message: first the Christian schools, then the churches. Suddenly a new spirit of moral activism was born among the ministers of our nation; through them, it will permeate church members and influence the millions of other pro-moral citizens who demand, "This is *our* country."

Californians for Biblical Morality

For California ministers, the spark that stirred them to action was the failure of proposition six at the polls. This constitutional initiative would have made it clear that California school boards could fire homosexual teachers. Unfortunately, it was not worded to best advantage and was underfinanced. In addition, the churches were totally disorganized. Consequently, the proposition was unable to withstand the massive attacks mounted against it by the media, humanist educators, and liberal politicians.

Along with other pastors, I was deeply concerned. After considerable prayer and contemplation, I invited the pastors of the largest churches in our state to attend a meeting in Fresno, the approximate center of our 800-mile state. Thirty-two pastors from many denominations, attended, representing some of the fastest growing churches in the country. Because of our unanimous concern, we developed a counterattack. The only individuals who can lead the moral majority in our state to halt the juggernaut advance of amoral humanism are the millions of church people. However, they will not follow politicians; they respond only to the leadership of their pastor-shepherds. Knowing pastors as we did, we all recognized that the only way to organize them was to make it clear that our basis of cooperation was moral, not theological, and to launch an organization led by pastors, operated by pastors, and subject to pastoral control. They would then lead their people to work as moral activists.

The initial body picked 10 ministers, well-known throughout the state, to serve on our executive committee. I am happy to report that these busy men were so concerned with the need for a moral voice in our state that each one accepted the first invitation to serve. Shortly afterward, 110 influential pastors were asked to join our administrative committee, knowing that their names would be carried on our letterhead. Of the 110, 90 accepted. A pastor was elected executive secretary, an office was opened, a monthly newsletter was inaugurated, and a recruitment campaign has been launched to secure 1,000 more pastor members. By the time this book is published, we will have at least 1,100 pastor members and will have instituted our "100,000 moral activists" membership drive, which will reach 1 million members by 1984. The pastors of California are serious about the fact that amoral humanism must be stopped! And you can be sure that California's political leaders are going to hear from their constituency whenever they consider moral and family issues. Too long, Hollywood has set the tone for morality in our state. We believe it is time for the approximately 5 million church members and an equal number of other pro-moralists to determine that standard.

The Moral Majority, Inc.

Dr. Jerry Falwell, pastor of one of the largest churches in the country, is, in my opnion, the most influential minister in America. He is watched each Sunday by over 15 million people, has founded Liberty Baptist College, holds conferences and seminars for thousands of ministers annually, and conducts the largest God-and-Country rallies in the nation. Several times, he mentioned to me the need to start an organization that could reach the 110,000 Bible-believing pastors in the country, in order to awaken the millions of sleeping moralists who are interested but uncommitted. After reviewing a "Clean Up America Survey" in TV guides and newspapers, he was convinced by the responses of over 2 million people that a sleeping giant was out there, waiting for someone to lead them, anxious to do something before it was too late to stop the destruction of our nation.

Dr. Greg Dixon, pastor of the Indianapolis Baptist Temple, and I were asked by Dr. Falwell to serve on the board of directors of Moral Majority, Inc. Dr. Bob Billings, past president of Hyles-Anderson College in Hammond, Indiana, has become the executive director. Later, Dr. James Kennedy, famous soul-winning Presbyterian pastor of Coral Ridge Presbyterian Church of Fort Lauderdale, Florida, and Dr. Charles Stanley, pastor of the First Baptist Church of Atlanta, Georgia, were added to the board. Upon opening an office in Washington, D.C., we have compiled a list of 80,000 pastors and begun a biweekly newspaper, to keep pastors and their people informed of pro-moral, prolife, profamily, and pro-American issues as they arise.

The first appeal for funds that went out from Moral Majority, Inc. told the recipient four times that his gift was not tax deductible, but people were so concerned for their country that they responded anyway. Our goal is to start a Moral Majority chapter in every state in the union. Five area field men, in charge of ten states each, are already actively organizing. We have launched a nationwide voter-registration drive, in response to recent surveys that indicate there are over 8 to 10 million unregistered voters in our country. That is a sin! If all the Christians in America voted for the presidential candidate who took the strongest stand on morality and defense of the family, we could easily make the difference in the next election. Both presidents Kennedy and Carter won their election by margins of less than 2 million votes. Gallup says there are 60 million Christians 18 years old and over!

Several of the outstanding pastors in America have agreed to help us conduct seminars for pastors throughout the land, in the greatest attempt ever made to encourage ministers and Christians to stand up and speak out against the further erosion of our moral fiber. Dr. Falwell is quoted in one of the leading secular magazines as predicting that "During the next ten or fifteen years, Bible-believing ministers will become the most influential leaders in the country." (Those interested in receiving more information about the Moral Majority or receiving the Moral Majority report may write Moral Majority Inc., 420 C. Street, N.E. Washington, D.C. 20002.)

To those who insist that ministers ought not get involved in politics, I would propose two explanations: We wouldn't have to, if politicians would confine themselves to government, economics, and national defense, but today they are intruding into areas of morality and the family, attempting to legislate outside their domain. We would do well to study the message of John the Baptist and the prophet Jonah, who cried out, "Repent or perish." The ministries of Daniel, Ezekiel, Jeremiah, and other prophets greatly affected the political spheres of their day.

It is time that our nation's leaders consult Bible-believing ministers, who represent the largest single group in America, instead of the directors of the Gay Rights Task Force or NOW or other amoral special-interest groups. That will only happen if we vote out of office all those whose voting records prove they are amoral or are confused about morality, replacing them with individuals who are openly biblical on moral and family issues.

The number of ministers who feel this way is growing rapidly. In fact, I have attended meetings in Washington where pastors of the largest churches, denominations, and church groups have expressed the same concern. At one such meeting, it was pointed out that "The sixty million born-again Christians are totally ignored by our government leaders. We are the largest minority in the country [one in five adults, according to Gallup], yet not one cabinet member or high-level government appointee is known to be born again." That certainly is not because we lack qualified personnel to offer for government service.

Christian leaders are rapidly beginning to realize that the Christian community has a tremendous amount of potential to offer our country, both morally and governmentally. The coming two decades will see many of them serving God by actively serving our country. America didn't hesitate to call on us during wartime, and the battle that engages us today is far more dangerous to the nation than any we have known before.

Concerned Women for America

In the fall of 1978, my wife, Beverly, was invited to speak at a prolife rally in San Diego. While waiting her turn to address the group, she listened to concerned women talk about the sinful crimes of abortion being perpetrated locally and nationally. They also discussed the dangers of the Equal Rights Amendment to the family. Recognizing that these women had correctly assessed the situation, she was shocked to discover that, although our church is the largest in the city, she did not recognize any of our members in the audience. Not only were our ladies absent, but so were women from the other Bible-teaching churches. She met many deeply concerned Catholic ladies, several Mormons, but almost no Protestants.

A few days later, one of the humanist leaders of the National Organization of Women (NOW) was quoted as speaking "for the women of America" in her endorsement of the ERA. Bev looked at me and protested, "She doesn't speak for me! And she doesn't represent millions of other women, either." She contacted three other ministers' wives on our staff. The ladies organized a rally, selected five other women, incorporated Concerned Women for America, and launched a national prayer-chain campaign and a monthly newsletter. In their first year, they have gathered over 94,000 members and are pursuing a goal of over 150,000. Already prayer chapters are springing up in every state, and in the near future, they will be found in all major cities. I have started a number of organizations, all of which enjoy substantial growth, but I have never seen anything like this! The moral-minded women of America are indeed concerned. (Those interested in CWA should write Beverly LaHaye, P.O. Box 20376, El Cajon, CA. 92021.)

A Myriad of Profamily Organizations

The above organizations are mentioned because I am intimately involved with them. But many other groups are springing up throughout the nation. They represent different religious preferences and a variety of special interests, but all share a deep, common concern for preserving the family and returning the nation to moral sanity.

One of the oldest groups is the Pro-Life Movement, predominantly Catholic in its origin but now including concerned people from all religious backgrounds, many from the medical profession. They have probably done more than anyone to awaken Americans to the devastating number of murders perpetrated in this country since the harmful United States Supreme Court decision of January 22, 1973, granting a woman the "right" to murder her unborn child at any time. (Of course, instead of calling it murder, they utilize the euphemism *abortion,* which makes it more palatable.) The Pro-Life movement, which has already successfully removed some proabortion senators and congressmen, is not sectarian and is endorsed by citizens of good will from all religious groups, who share their concern for the growing holocaust of abortion-on-demand. Another effective organization is Eagle Forum, founded by Phyllis Schlafly, a mother, lawyer, and articulate prolife and profamily patriot. This organization has done more to stop the ERA from passage than any other single group. In the process, it has helped educate millions of our citizens, resulting in a healthy proliferation of pro-moral, profamily groups, many of which I must risk insulting by omission, not because they lack effectiveness, but because I lack space in this book.

Family America

In early 1979, Bev and I were asked to be cochairmen of a new organization called Family America. We accepted because of their central objective, not because we wanted something else to do. FA is an organization of organizations, serving as a clearinghouse for the many pro-moral, family-oriented groups starting up. Our purpose is to supply information to all member groups about what other like-minded groups are doing, so our activities can be orchestrated to increase their effectiveness. What I expected to be a little operation, with an office in Washington servicing 15–25 organizations, within its first year has begun sending materials regularly to over 100 groups throughout the country. All of them have members, a sphere of influence, and a deep concern about saving America from the chaos that is certain to come upon us, if we permit the humanists in government to run our country.

These organizations will be successful, with God's help, *if* we are united in getting our message out to a sufficient number of people.

The Bible says, "My people are destroyed for lack of knowledge . . ." Hosea 4:6.

Americans are being destroyed because they do not really know the voting records of their politicians or the moral principles of their candidates. Part of the educational commitment of these organizations is to acquaint sufficient numbers of our citizens with the facts, so we can send elected officials into all positions of government as representatives of America's moral majority. We must transmit an urgent message to these leaders: We will be watching their every vote—particularly on morals, preservation of life, the family, and other issues that represent the best interests of the United States.

11

Separation of
Church and State

One of the chief reasons for the apathy of so many Christians today, particularly ministers, is a misunderstanding of an important concept: separation of church and state. By no stretch of the imagination was that doctrine ever meant to separate government from God. But if the church withdraws from all government involvement, that is exactly what will result.

When I was in Moscow, our guide proudly proclaimed, "We Russians have the same policy on religion as you Americans—separation of church and state." Suddenly I began to realize what an overemphasis on that concept would do for America. The state in Russia is everything, and the church is irrelevant. The influence of the church in Russia is almost zero.

We are headed for the same predicament. Every week that passes finds the state politicizing something new. First it was taxes, national defense, and education; now morals, the family, and other nonconstitutional issues seem to fall within the domain of government.

The humanist view of government cries, "Bigger is better!" or, "Whatever needs to be done, government can do it better." Consequently, government is gradually reaching its sticky fingers into everything. If the present interpretation of church-state separation is followed, the church will soon be excluded from everything meaningful in our lives.

During a TV debate on homosexual rights, my opponent brought up the church-state issue. "The church shouldn't get involved in politics. It will endanger its tax status." That is ridiculous, by any legal definition. In the first place, morals are the church's business. If the church doesn't speak out on homosexuality, pornography, prostitution, abortion, divorce, and so forth, who will? Assuredly, preaching the Gospel is the primary business of the church, but being the salt of the earth certainly includes asserting a moral influence, and today those morals have been politicized by the humanists.

At the 1979 NOW (National Organization of Women) convention in Los Angeles, the feminist leaders warned their delegates of the rise of the moral majority, who were rapidly awakening from their slumber to become moral activitists. They challenged their followers to solve the problem by going home and threatening the Christians with "The separation-of-church-and-state issue." Obviously they did not care a snap about the church, but they wanted to neutralize its influence, so they could continue to flood our land with "homosexual rights," "lebian rights," "prostitute rights," and "abortion rights." What humanists call *rights,* the church consistently calls *wrongs.* Therefore, if we fail to get involved politically on these moral issues, the humanists will pollute our land.

Washington attorney Alan Dye and my San Diego attorney friend, James O. Hewitt, both highly respected lawyers, have issued lengthy papers on the church's rights under the law. Both acknowledge that churches may not endorse political candidates or give money to political campaigns, without jeopardizing their nonprofit status. But when it comes to legislative activity—that is, campaigning for or against legislation under consideration, particularly when it concerns morals—churches are permitted to be involved, as long as they do not spend a substantial amount of time or money in the process. *Substantial* is generally considered anything over 5 percent of their annual budget or 5 percent of their activity. (As private citizens, ministers are not prohibited from endorsing candidates. A copy of this legal brief will be sent on request to any pastor who writes Moral Majority, Inc., 420 C Street, N.E. Washington, D.C., 20002.) Even the most politically active of churches would probably not spend ½ of 1 percent. Consequently, most churches are functioning well within the limits of the law.

Many, however, heed the big lie that churches should never get involved in politics. Although churches should not officially endorse candidates for public office, that does not mean that Christians should not run for public office or that churches should not speak out clearly on moral issues. A chief reason that 8 million babies have been murdered in the past few years and that homosexuality, pornography, and sexual immorality are flooding our land, is the deafening silence of the churches.

This nation was not founded independently of God. Our money carries the message "In God We Trust," and our Pledge of Allegiance states that we are "one nation under God." Our Supreme Court, Senate, and House of Representatives open each morning with prayer. This country was built on biblical principles and a clear recognition of God. But atheistic, amoral humanists have moved in, until they control our nation's destiny and are seeking to separate her from God. This is particularly true of our judges, a high percentage of whom make humanistic decisions. Because most judgeships are appointed positions, it will take several years to change that picture. The only way to bring morality back into our judicial system is to elect strong, pro-moral candidates to all federal offices, particularly in the key positions of president, senator, and state governor. Remember, most federal judges are appointed by the president on the recommendation of the senators from his party, and a similar approach is used for lesser judicial posts.

One aspect of Governor Ronald Reagan's leadership in California that I particularly appreciated was his high moral standards in appointing judges. What little legal moral sanity we have left in California can be attributed largely to those judges still in office as a result of appointments made during the eight-year Reagan administration. His successor has not followed those policies, as everyone knows, accounting for a rapidly declining moral trend in our state. In fact, Governor Jerry Brown was the first official in American history to knowingly appoint an acknowledged homosexual judge, which showed his total disrespect for traditional moral values. Like every other pro-moral American, I shuddered when, during his second presidential campaign, he announced that what he had done for the homosexuals of California, he would, if elected president, do for the entire country. If there is anything America does not need, it is more amoral humanists appointed or elected to govern pro-moral citizens. Elected officials, not the citizens of our country, are primarily responsible for polluting our country. They need to be replaced, regardless of party by pro-moralists.

The Truth About
Separation of Church and State

The First Amendment of our Constitution reads, "Congress shall make no law respecting an establishment of religion, or prohibiting the free exercise thereof; or abridging the freedom of speech, or of the press; or the right of the people peaceably to assemble, and to petition the Government for a redress of grievances."

Our forefathers never intended government to be isolated from God or the recognition of His existence. By constantly threatening Christians with the false interpretation of separation, the humanists have now rendered our government almost as secular as Russia's. They are even beginning to duplicate their successes in education—that is, expelling religion from the schools, equating morals with religion, and thus including morals in the expulsion. We have already seen that morals and religion have no place in the humanist's scheme of education. The same concept is now working in government: First, separate religion and politics, then equate religion and morals, and subsequently exclude both.

The separation of church and state does not mean that Christian citizens are prohibited from taking an active part in the electoral process. Our forefathers were simply preventing the establishment of a state religion, which Europe had endured for centuries. Even today, for instance, we find a state or government-supported church in Germany and England.

Is it conceivable that America could institute a state-controlled religion? The foundation is already being laid. Until 1979, we did not have a tax-supported religion in America. Instead, all religions were free to operate within the framework of minimal legal guidelines. But that changed in 1979, for during that year, under the guidance of a well-publicized born-again president, the federal government established a Department of Education with a $40 billion budget. Since the educational system has been taken over by humanism, and since humanism is an officially declared religion, we find the government establishing a religion and giving the high priest a position in the president's cabinet.

Ironically, the taxes to pay for the establishment of such a godless religion come from people who are overwhelmingly God conscious and pro-moral. Particularly is that true when the humanist "change agents" of education brainwash the captive children in our federal schools with their amoral religious beliefs. If you think that a bit strong, you have not read *The Change Agents,* by Barbara Morris. She points out that the individuals we used to call schoolteachers are now social "change agents." Their goal is to modify the morals of our nation's schoolchildren. They are more interested in morals modification (which they subtlely call "values clarification") than they are in academic standards and good learning. Does that sound frightening? It is!

Our Lord warned that it would be better for one who destroyed the minds of children to hang a millstone around his neck and jump into the sea. I believe it is equally repulsive for Christians to sit back and do nothing while such religious brainwashing takes place. Unless 60 million of us become vitally involved in changing our present humanistic leadership, America will be a humanist nation by the twenty-first century.

While attending a meeting of concerned ministers and other Christian leaders in Washington a few weeks ago, I met an attorney from Memphis. He had his eyes opened while serving as a federal prosecutor during some hard-core-pornography trials that occurred in his city. Pornography is a $4 billion business, so obviously its publishers can afford the sharpest humanist lawyers in the nation. After battling them for almost three years, this attorney raised an overriding question: "Where are all the Christians who say they are in opposition to iniquity?" He concluded, "I believe that pornography floods our land because the Christians refuse to 'get involved' in fighting it." I would only add to that point one further observation: Next to abortion, pornography is the most contaminating scourge in our country.

How long can the Christian community remain silent?

One Church's Moral Activism

Pastor Marvin Rickard is a warm, personal friend. As a fellow pastor, I admire him greatly. He is the minister of the Los Gatos Christian Church, the largest church in northern California. I held a week of meetings in that church, when they averaged an attendance of 700 in morning services. Today they average more than 5,000. Marvin is a fundamental, Bible-teaching, missionary-minded, soul-winning man of God, who emphasizes the Spirit-filled life to his congregation. He is also deeply concerned about the declining moral standards of our state, which is why he serves with me and eight other pastors on the executive committee of the Californians for Biblical Morality, a group of over 1,100 ministers who share his concern.

During the summer of 1979, the Human Relations Committee (with guidance from the federal government) recommended to the Santa Clara County Board of Supervisors the passage of a special ordinance, striking down the centuries-old laws regarding discrimination on the basis of sexual choice. This kind of legislation, which is cropping up all over the country (at federal insistence), assumes (without any scientific evidence) that homosexuals are born the way they are, and it would put homosexuals, blacks, Chicanos, Indians, and left-handed people in the same category. This, of course, is an insult to all races, for homosexuality—a learned behavior, rather than a genetic product—is reversible.

Over 800 people from several churches attended 25 hours of testimony. Letters from the presidents of the largest corporations in the county stated their opposition to this action. Once such legislation is passed, some liberal, humanist judge can rule that quotas must be followed, and these corporations did not want to fire heterosexual employees in order to make room for homosexuals. Another problem concerns rentals. If such a law is passed, a duplex owner with three sons, who lives next door to his rental, could not refuse to rent to a homosexual. In addition, schoolteachers could not be fired for being homosexuals, and, as I point out in my book *The Unhappy Gays,* that is deplorable! Whenever homosexual teachers are allowed to exalt homosexuality as an optional life-style to prepubertal children, the homosexual population will double in ten years.

At one point in the discussion, Marvin rose to speak, and a

5.3-scale earthquake occurred. The supervisors were flabbergasted by the spontaneous cheers and applause of the church people. Marvin then explained that the Bible records several cases in which God has sent earthquakes at a time of judgment on depravity. In spite of that and a warning that their action was opposed to community moral standards, the committee approved the proposal by a vote of 4 to 1.

The church people of that community banded together, formed a moral coalition, and organized a petition drive, with over 2,000 participating. They needed 37,000 signatures, in order to nullify the supervisors' action by having it placed on the following year's ballot. In two weeks, they collected over 50,000 signatures.

Within a month, the city council of San Jose, the largest city in Santa Clara County, passed a similar ordinance. Since only 18,000 signatures were required to overturn it, opponents secured over 25,000, killing the action for one year, until the entire electorate can make a choice. During the interim, the pro-moral citizens will be able to voice their concerns to a broad constituency.

Christians who criticize their fellow believers in Santa Clara County are morally asleep. Fortunately, the majority of Christians are awakening to the realization that America was once based on moral sanity and that it is wrong to let a noisy minority put pressure on amoral or politically opportunistic politicians to pass laws removing our much-needed moral safeguards. Because man is not good by nature, a civilized culture must have moral laws based on biblical absolutes. Otherwise, chaos will ensue.

On behalf of the Christians of San Diego County, I would like to publicly thank the Christians of Santa Clara County for their efforts. Two months after their courageous defense of morality, our county supervisors announced they were considering the same type of legislation. When I first read about this in the paper, I sent a letter to each of the supervisors, with a copy of my book on homosexuality. Subsequently, I have spoken with three of them, all of whom had heard of the turmoil in the north. Consequently, although they had already given assurance to the homosexuals and other radical pressure groups that they would pass something, it has been modified drastically, to apply only to county employees. Doubtless, the pro-moral majority in many other counties across the state is indebted to our patriotic, moral citizens in Santa Clara County.

Such moral activism would never be necessary, if Christians and pro-moral citizens would get involved with the electoral process as candidates and workers for good candidates. I am convinced that every Christian who does not feel led of God to run for public office ought to work for and contribute to the campaign of candidates who share his moral convictions. If we did, we could solve most of America's moral ills in a single decade. That isn't politics; it is just good Christian citizenship.

12

Is Humanist Tribulation Necessary?

Most knowledgeable Christians are looking for the Second Coming of Christ and the tribulation period that He predicted would come before the end of the age. Because present world conditions are so similar to those the Bible prophesies for the last days (*see* 2 Timothy 3:1–7; 2 Peter 3:1–15; Matthew 24:6, 7, 37, 38), they conclude that a takeover of our culture by the forces of evil is inevitable; so they do nothing to resist it. This is unscriptural! We are commanded to resist the devil and to put on the whole armor of God, that we may be able to withstand in the evil day (*see* Ephesians 6:13).

Unfortunately, many Christians who are alarmed by the flood of humanism outlined in this book assume that they should do nothing to stop it. Some say, "It is inevitable that perilous times shall come as we approach the end of the age," so they are unwilling to raise their voices or vote. They have resigned themselves to tribulation.

The seven-year tribulation period will be a time that features the rule of the anti-Christ over the world. I cover this extensively in my book *The Beginning of the End*. It originates with the signing of a covenant between Israel and the anti-Christ, which he breaks after three and one-half years. That tribulation is predestined and will surely come to pass. But the pre-tribulation tribulation—that is, the tribulation that will engulf this country if liberal humanists are permitted to take total control of our government—is neither predestined nor necessary. But it will deluge the entire land in the next few years, unless Christians are willing to become much more assertive in defense of morality and decency than they have been during the past three decades.

I am not blind to the fact that world conditions are depraved. Adultery, pornography, and homosexuality are rampant, and, as the Bible predicted, people are " . . . lovers of themselves, boastful, proud, blasphemers, disobedient to parents, unthankful, unholy, unloving, unforgiving, without self-control, brutal, despisers of those that are good, headstrong, haughty and lovers of pleasure rather than lovers of God" (2 Timothy 3:2–4). That sounds like the front page of the daily newspaper, doesn't it?

But such a condition does not have to exist in every country in the world as we prepare for the coming of Christ. Before the anti-Christ appears on the scene to set up his depraved kingdom, Russia will be destroyed by God for attacking Israel (Ezekiel 38, 39. *See* author's detailed explanation of these coming events in *The Beginning of the End*). The Hebrew prophets foresaw a Western confederation of nations that would mildly oppose Russia. America, Canada, England, a section of Europe, and Australia form part of that Western confederation. But *there is no prophetic requirement that this Western confederation be in a state of moral tribulation before that day*—which comes just prior to the tribulation period.

Today Sweden may be closer to pretribulation conditions than any other nation in the Western world. Not because it was predestined, but because the godly Christians and pro-moral citizens did nothing to stop the socialist, humanist takeover of their government. Consequently, they have turned that delightful land into Sodom and Gomorrah. Remember Dr. Schaeffer's warning that humanism always leads to chaos.

It may be too late for the Christians in Sweden to oust the humanists from office, but it certainly is not too late in America and Canada, and there may still be time to save England and Australia.

The International Soul Harvest

My wife and I have traveled in forty-four countries of the world, including five Communist nations. Christianity is not dying! It may surprise you to know that this is a day that is experiencing a mighty moving of the Holy Spirit. The humanistically controlled press says little about it, but Christianity is on the rise, all over the world. Missionaries report that Third World countries, in spite of repressive regimes, oppressive inflation, and starvation conditions, are turning to Christ in unprecedented numbers. For two decades, great numbers of people have been finding Christ in South America. Missionaries in Europe indicate a renewed interest in the Gospel. One missionary in France told me that more were converted to Christ last year than had been saved in the first eleven years he was there. I could tell you of the work of God in India, Singapore, Korea, Taiwan, and even behind the Iron and Bamboo Curtains. Reports coming out of both Russia and China indicate a surprising thirst for Christ on the part of the young.

Yes, Christianity is growing worldwide—not dying. We cannot assess its growth for sure, of course, but I would estimate that Christianity has more than doubled in the last 25 years. In fact, just 20 years ago, the humanists thought they had stifled the church in America by gaining control of the National Council of Churches. But they had not reckoned with the power of the Holy Spirit to work through the Bible-believing fundamental churches throughout the land, which have grown enormously during that period. After World War II, most of the large churches were liberal. But these apostates have suffered a great decline, whereas the fundamental churches have flourished to such a degree that almost every city in the land has a dynamic, Bible-believing church. In California alone, I know of 6 churches whose services' average attendance is close to 5,000 each Sunday. It shouldn't have surprised us when George Gallup announced that over 60 million people in America claim to have had a born-again experience with Jesus Christ. After all, Bible-teaching churches are faithfully proclaiming the Word of God.

Church growth is not the only fact declaring that Christianity is alive and well. The fastest growing movement in the nation is that of Christian schools, kindergarten through twelfth grade. That is why the humanists tried in 1979 to use the IRS to harass Christian schools and make it more difficult to start new ones. They see this movement as a threat to their control of young minds through humanistic false beliefs and theories.

Christian booksellers are publishing millions of books each year, providing such an impressive alternative to humanistic fallacies that secular book companies want to buy them out. The last time I attended a Christian bookseller's convention, I was approached by four secular publishers about writing a book for them, three of whom had agents there, inquiring as to whether any of the publishers were for sale. When that happens, you can be sure that Christian publishing is profitable; this can also mean that we are getting our message out, in spite of the humanistic control of the newsstands and bookstores, which often refuse to carry Christian literature.

Another powerful factor in the great soul harvest of recent years is the new openness on the part of Christians to effectively share their faith in Christ to almost every individual they meet. Dr. Bill Bright, who founded Campus Crusade for Christ, can largely be credited with spearheading the training of thousands of individual Christians, who are storming the spiritual wastelands of humanistic college campuses, leading students by the hundreds of thousands to Christ. Dr. Jack Hyles, pastor of the 25,000 member First Baptist Church of Hammond, Indiana, together with the famous evangelist Dr. John R. Rice, editor of the *Sword of the Lord,* mailed to 50,000 subscribers each week, have held hundreds of "soul-winning conferences" throughout the country, training thousands of church people how to lead others to Christ. When I was a boy, I didn't know anyone who was able to share his faith effectively. The Gallup Poll indicated that 25 million Christians have already tried to share their faith with at least one other individual. That clearly indicates that the number of Christians in America could well double in the next decade!

One reason I am anticipating another decade of soul harvest is that we are experiencing a refreshing movement of the Holy Spirit in many of our congregations today. Churches that one or two decades ago were spiritually dead have come to life, and the Spirit-controlled life-style they teach has injected a new vitality and joy into them, which is contagious. Christian families are experiencing outstanding instruction on family living and interpersonal relationships, all biblically based. Consequently, their happiness and fulfillment in life is unsurpassed. This increased stability and joy has not gone unnoticed by the many victims of humanistic education, whose families are often filled with hostility, violence, and infidelity. Many such victims of our times are looking to the church for the answers to the breakdown of the home caused by the humanistic insanity that is constantly assaulting the family. (The author is not unaware that divorce and immorality have increased within the church today because many ill-advised Christians have heeded the temptations of humanism, reaping the misery it eventually produces. By contrast, those who are really seeking God's will in their lives possess better learning tools than most of us did when starting out thirty years ago.)

The utter bankruptcy of humanism is rapidly coming to

light today, causing many to return to basics—and that often means the church and biblical principles for living. Unfortunately, the futility and hopelessness that humanistic existentialism engenders often leads to suicide, cults, TM, or other equally empty fads. However, many thousands are turning to Christ. Never have I seen a better time for effectively sharing one's faith than today. By the year 1990, I expect 40 percent of all Americans to profess a personal faith in Christ and over 51 percent of all educable schoolchildren to be attending Christian or private schools. That will occur if the humanists can be stymied in their assault on morality, the family, parents' rights, and our time-honored freedoms. Spirit-filled salty Christians during this decade will reap an unusual harvest.

A Question of Motivation

Those who read this may question my real motivation, for this book certainly is different from all my others. Why would a pastor so vigorously attack the religion of humanism? Is it primarily patriotic love for my country? Not really. I am patriotic, but that is not my dominant concern. You must understand; I am first and foremost a committed Christian. As such, I have a command to preach the Gospel to every creature. That is my number-one priority. Since my wife and I have traveled around the world, have spoken face-to-face with over 16 percent of the world's faithful missionaries, and have visited the largest Christian radio stations in the world, which preach Christ's message of salvation in the major languages of the world, we have recognized a fundamental fact: 80 to 85 percent of the world's missionaries, technology for preaching the Gospel, and money for world missions comes from America. If the atheistic, amoral, one-world humanists succeed in enslaving our country, that missionary outlet will eventually be terminated. As a Christian and as a pastor, I am deeply concerned that this ministry be extended. The eternal souls of millions of people depend on us to supply them with the good news. In addition, I am concerned that the 50 million children who will grow up in America during the next generation will have access to the truth, rather than the heresies of humanism.

God has richly blessed my writing ministry, with over 300,000 copies of my books being sold each year. These serve as a portion of my pastoral ministry to American believers. I sincerely pray that God will use this book to activate my readers to defend our nation's morals. If other ministers of the Gospel will use their sphere of influence, whether great or small, to similarly roll back the tidal waves of humanist thought in our country, we can yet win the battle for the mind. That will ultimately result in the salvation of millions of the most precious thing in the universe—the souls of people.

Personally, I believe it is worth the fight! If you agree, read the next chapter and ask God what He would have you do.

13

What You Can Do

Do not ask what America can do for you;
ask what you can do for America!
John F. Kennedy

If America is going to be saved from the humanist onslaught described in this book, it will take the combined efforts of the pro-moral majority, particularly the Christian community. The Gallup Poll claims there are 100 million adult church and synagogue members, 31 million of whom are evangelical. We evangelicals are certainly not the only ones interested in morality and the family, but we most likely will be motivated to speak out on these issues. If we do, millions of other pro-moralists will follow. Many in liberal churches, who are sick of the humanism in their denominations, will gladly follow our lead, if they can but hear our voice. That is why no one man or group of men can do it alone.

We are in a battle—and it takes armies to win wars. We need an army of moral activists, led by their Bible-believing ministers, who will provide America with the moral leadership for which this country hungers.

You are only one person, but you are one! You cannot make the decision for 60 million, but you can decide, with God's help, to use whatever talent and effort you possess in the time we have left to turn this country around. The following 12 suggestions are given in their order of importance. Please evaluate them carefully.

Pray!

If my people, which are called by my name, shall humble themselves, and pray, and seek my face, and turn from their wicked ways; then will I hear from heaven, and will forgive their sin, and will heal their land.

2 Chronicles 7:14

Benjamin Franklin was right when he said . . .

I have lived, Sir, a long time; and the longer I live the more convincing Proofs I see of this Truth, That God governs in the Affairs of Men!—And if a Sparrow cannot fall to the Ground without his Notice, is it probable that an Empire can rise without his Aid?—We have been assured, Sir, in the Sacred Writings, that "except the Lord build the House, they labor in vain that build it." I firmly believe this;—and I also believe that without his concurring Aid we shall succeed in this political Building no better than the Builders of Babel: . . .

I therefore beg leave to move, That henceforth Prayers, imploring the Assistance of Heaven, and its Blessing on our Deliberations, be held in this Assembly every Morning before we proceed to Business . . . [139]

Benjamin Franklin
Constitutional Convention
Philadelphia
June 28, 1787

Pray for the Key Sixteen   Although you have probably prayed for America many times, have you specifically entreated the Lord for the sixteen people whom you elect to office—those

KEY 16
Prayer List

"Prayers, intercessions and giving of thanks be made for. . .all who are in authority, that we may lead a quiet and peaceable life in all godliness and reverence." I Tim. 2:1-2

U.S. GOVERNMENT FIVE

PRESIDENT_____

VICE PRESIDENT_____

U.S SENATOR_____

U.S. SENATOR_____

CONGRESSMAN_____

STATE GOVERNMENT FIVE

GOVERNOR_____

LT. GOVERNOR_____

ATTORNEY GENERAL_____

STATE SENATOR_____

ASSEMBLYMAN_____

LOCAL GOVERNMENT SIX

MAYOR_____

CITY COUNCILMAN_____

CITY ATTORNEY_____

SCHOOL BOARD_____

COUNTY SUPERVISOR_____

SHERIFF_____

These 16 officials whom we elect and whose salaries we pay through our taxes, determine the moral standards of our community. As a good citizen, pray that wisdom and courage will be granted to them and let them know your feelings, particularly on moral issues, that they will provide the next generation a morally sane society.

who determine the moral tone of your community and nation? It may surprise you that praying for those in authority over you, which is a command of Scripture, is not as overwhelming a task as you might think. Did you realize that you only elect five people nationally, five in your state, and six locally, to represent you in government? You pay their salaries through your taxes—and they make the decisions that largely determine how you and your children will live—but do you pray for them?

(Those interested in a free "Key 16" prayer card may write Concerned Women for America, P.O. Box 20376, El Cajon, CA. 92021.) Examine the following:

Our church and Concerned Women for America challenge their members to pray daily for these key sixteen leaders. You can do the same in your area.

Therefore I exhort first of all that supplications, prayers, intercessions, and giving of thanks be made for all men, for kings and all who are in authority, that we may lead a quiet and peaceable life in all godliness and reverence. For this is good and acceptable in the sight of God our Savior, who desires all men to be saved and to come to the knowledge of the truth.

1 Timothy 2:1–4 NKJB-NT

Continue Sharing Your Faith

Gallup suggests that 50 percent of the 31 million evangelicals share their faith once a week; 5 million do so once or more daily. If the rest of our evangelicals would share their faith effectively, we could easily solve the moral problems of our age by sheer numbers of converts.

The next two decades will provide an unprecedented opportunity for Christians to disseminate their faith in Christ personally, for two primary reasons: Humanism has brought about so much moral and civil chaos that people are looking for something real to believe in; and as we approach the end of this century, there will be an increasing apprehension that something catastrophic is going to happen before the year 2,000. Some expect the increase in earthquakes to produce one gigantic upheaval; others fear the encirclement of the Free World by Communism, the proliferation of nuclear capability, expansion of terrorist groups, and many other unsettling possibilities. The uncertainty of these possibilities and the futility of humanism is fertile ground for those who have "the truth as it is in Christ Jesus." In Him we have the answer to troubled hearts; let's not keep it to ourselves.

Continue to Show Your Concern
And Compassion for Humanism's Victims

Christians have historically been the most humanitarian of people. We are taught by our Lord to care deeply for others. The story of the Good Samaritan needs reenactment in daily living. We need to assist the poor, the refugees, and the troubled victims of humanism's libertine concepts. We are impelled to cry out against abortion and adultery, but we must also reach out loving arms to unwed mothers, divorced partners, and children being raised by one parent.

Thank God for those Christian men who lovingly shared some of their time and energy with my brother and me, after the death of our father, providing the proper role models we desperately needed during such a crossroads experience. Just because there are so many single parents today is no reason to neglect them.

Concerned Women for America has taken a strong position against abortion, ERA, and other so-called human-rights issues. In addition, though a relatively new organization, they are trying to put together a local abortion-counseling program for unwed mothers, so that young girls can receive the proper kind of love and advice during their time of need. Most government-controlled programs render standard humanist advice: "Abort; it's your body." Concerned citizens should provide moral and emotional support as these girls cope with the biggest decision of their lives.

I hope this counseling ministry will follow CWA's prayer chains all over the country.

Promote the National Drive
To Register Christians

We have already pointed out that between 8 and 10 million Christians are not even registered to vote. Every Bible-teaching church should designate at least one special Christian Citizenship Sunday for registration of all members. This is nonpartisan, nonpolitical, positive citizenship, so it should be pursued with diligence.

After being registered, offer to become the registrar of voters for your church. After a short period of training, you can help others prepare for election day.

The importance of registering millions of Christians and enabling them to exercise their God-given right to vote for their country's leaders cannot be overemphasized. A political forecaster indicated that fewer people are going to the polls than ever before, and that phenomenon is expected to get worse in the 1980s. He then confirmed that cities in New York, New Jersey, and Connecticut had recently elected officials with less than 25 percent of the vote.

We can understand why the general population is disillusioned with politicians. They seem so different after being elected, so unresponsive to the people who elected them, cooperating instead with amoral activists and pressure groups. But such disillusionment only increases the effectiveness of the discerning, morally minded voter, who backs the candidate representing moral decency.

Volunteer to Help in the Campaign
Of Pro-Moral Candidates

Volunteer workers are the most significant single factor in winning elections on all levels—and that is often where Christians are the weakest. Few have the foresight to realize that a few weeks of work on behalf of the right candidate will save hours and years of humanistic turmoil—and even taxes.

According to former Congressman John Conlan, "three hundred precinct workers can elect almost any good candidate to Congress." With only 435 congressional districts, 120,500 of our 60 million Christians—a little more than one per church—could easily change the complexion of Congress in just one election. Now do you understand why I say we have been sound asleep?

One politician I know was converted while serving as a state assemblyman. After losing a bid for Congress, he ran the following year for mayor of one of the twenty largest cities in the country. With the heavy backing of the Christian community and others concerned for moral decency, he was elected. Today the porno shops of that city are closed, degenerate movies are not permitted, and other humanist trends have been halted. A sister city, just forty-five miles away, still features all of these things. What makes the difference? The office of the mayor—and who occupies it! If we are going to turn this country around, it will be at the voting booth. And since our press is so liberally dominated, usually endorsing those without moral values, we will have to make up the difference by a massive army of volunteer workers. We have more than enough manpower; now we need to activate it.

In many local elections, it is not difficult to get people elected. Citizens overlook the fact that many offices are won by only a few votes. For example, the governor of Ohio, who has worked energetically to get the humanists off the backs of Christian parents who send their children to Christian schools, was elected in 1973 by only a little over 11,000 votes. There are well over 1 million Christians eligible to vote in Ohio.

A deacon in a neighboring church announced his candidacy for a city-council seat. I invited a group of pastors to breakfast, to hear his testimony, and we organized an *ad hoc* group called Ministers Concerned for Moral Decency. Sixteen of us let our names be used to endorse that good man, as is our right as free citizens in this country. The letter was circulated far and wide, and he was elected by 691 votes. Even his opponent acknowledged that our letter was largely instrumental in the outcome. This year that man, a significant moral influence on our community, is running for mayor. His campaign was well worth our time and effort.

Expect Opposition   Whenever Christians and other morally minded citizens get involved in elections, the newspapers and humanist politicians get rather nervous. Our local paper blasted the councilman who was elected for bringing the church into his campaign. (Actually he didn't; he brought Christians into his campaign. Apparently they decided that one who becomes a Christian loses some of his citizen's rights.) Predictably, they waved the separation of church and state flag, because we ministers had endorsed him. That response always amuses me. They never raise that kind of objection when schoolteachers or homosexuals endorse candidates, or do they say a word when the feminists of NOW back a politician.

Evaluate Politicians Carefully   Christians seriously err when they insist that a candidate be a committed Christian before he is worthy of Christian support. We must learn that Christians are not the only ones with strong moral convictions. We need politicians sincerely committed to moral principles, with the character to stand up for them.

Personally, I would rather elect a man committed to biblical morality than one who loudly proclaims that he is a born-again Christian but refuses to define his moral position. For example, we have witnessed the presidency of a self-acknowledged, born-again leader who surrounded himself with amoral or immoral promoters during his campaign. When elected, he appointed most of these same people to office, together with a long list of humanists, who represent him in the administration of his government. As far as we know, he did not appoint one born-again Christian, or even an aggressive pro-moralist, to any major office. Men can be judged better by the company they keep and the kind of advisors they select than by their politically motivated statements of faith.

Morally minded people should heed one word of caution

with respect to politicians: Ignore what they say and carefully examine what they do. Remember, a professional politician or a humanist will say anything to get elected. His voting record speaks more loudly than his rhetoric, for it reveals what he really believes and it demonstrates how he responds to pressure.

Any elected official who has voted for abortion-on-demand, for ERA (and particularly the extension of ERA), for leniency on pornography, for decriminalization of prostitution, and for children's rights at the expense of parents' rights, is dangerous at best or amoral at worst. Consequently, he should be exposed and replaced at all costs, regardless of his party, race, or religion. Until we pro-moralists remove some of these people from office and return them to private life, where they will be less harmful to our culture, Washington, Sacramento, Albany, and other capitals will not take us seriously.

The only hope for America is that millions of the silent moral majority become militant about their morality and elect men of conviction and character to public office. If we are diligent in exercising our right and responsibility to vote such representatives into government leadership, the 1980s will be known as the Decade of Morality.

All politicians should be given "The Moral Minimums Test" (see Appendix A).

Work Vigorously to Expose Amoral Candidates and Incumbents

Carefully examine the voting record of the key sixteen who represent you or are candidates for those offices. Any who are "liberal," amoral, or weak on morality can be defeated, if you inform as many voters as possible what they really stand for. The media certainly won't expose their humanist views, for most papers and editors share them. Voters need to know the truth about politicians. A few hours spent in research and a few dollars invested at your local printer can render your community a favor by exposing amoral candidates to the light of the voting public.

In 1972, President Nixon was returned to the White House by an overwhelming margin—not because he was so popular, but because his opponent, Senator McGovern, had one of the most liberal voting records in the Senate. This clearly says to me that Americans, when they are fully informed of a man's platform, are not ready to vote in a leader who represents the moral values of a humanist. Yet just four years later, the voters elected a vice-president, only "a heartbeat away from the presidency," whose voting record in the Senate was worse than McGovern's.

How do you account for that? Did the morals of America change in four years? Not according to the Gallup Poll of 1979. No, the problem is exposure. It is hard for a presidential candidate to hide his true beliefs, but it is easier for all others to keep them from their constituency—including vice-presidential candidates.

One reason local politicians do not stay in office as long as national leaders is that the voters can keep better track of their voting records. National politicians often think we don't know what they are voting for. But since we have to live under their decisions, those of us who care should uncover their voting record, print it up, and circulate it. Every politician should be confronted with his voting record on Election Day—whether it is good or bad.

Become Informed and Enlighten Your Friends and Neighbors

It is important that you keep abreast of political events. The Moral Majority, Inc. newspaper will give you valuable national news, and your state Moral Majority group will provide you with area issues. Thoroughly understand the enemy for what he is and what he is doing to our country. Please consult the recommended reading list in Appendix B.

It is not enough to be informed personally. You should attempt to communicate pertinent information to your friends. Start with this book, and pass it on to a friend. Check to see if your pastor has read it. If not, make a gift of it, with the request that he read it. Instead of throwing away your pro-moral newsletters, loan them to your friends, duplicating key sections for those who need to know what is really taking place in our nation.

Some Christians fall into the malaise of thinking, "It's too late; there's no hope!" Nonsense! While we have freedom, let us use it to preserve our freedom. Someone has said, "It is better to light one little candle than to curse the darkness."

The right kind of book is a good candle.

Consider Running for Public Office

"Who me?" Yes, you. Every Christian should consider that possibility. Obviously, God doesn't want 60 million of us to run for office; but we could use 200,000. What are your qualifications? First, identify your moral convictions. After that, evaluate the office, the need, your speaking ability, and the coterie of friends who would help you. Start with small offices and work your way up. It is definitely something to pray about.

Join Local, State, and National Pro-Moral Organizations

Become active in one or more of the groups we have mentioned or others of like mind in your community. Christians have at times earned the reputation of "being so heavenly minded that they are no earthly good." The moral tone of the 1980s will be determined by the feminists, humanists, homosexuals, and liberals—or by pro-moral Christians. It is up to you.

If there is no group in your area, start one.

Speak Out and Write
Vigorously on Moral Issues

All government leaders are not deaf to the concerns of their constituencies. Several of our recent victories—i.e., stopping the ERA and the homosexual advance—have been due to letter-writing campaigns. Put each leader's address on your key sixteen prayer card, and let him hear from you on important moral, family-life, and national-defense issues.

This is a day of pressure politics. Unfortunately, the high-pressure tactics of the human-rights activists give our leaders the impression that they speak for the majority, when just the opposite is true. The only way to change that is to write concise, kind, respectful, but forthright letters, stipulating your reasons for favoring or opposing certain legislation or government activities. Such epistles are more effective than you think.

Contribute to Good, Pro-Moral Causes

It takes an enormous amount of money to fight amoral, government-backed legislation. Take ERA, for example. Five million federal dollars were provided for the Houston fiasco called the IWY (International Women's Year, an idea that originated in the Kremlin in Moscow, according to *U.S. News & World Report*). It turned out to be little more than a rallying call to pass the ERA. Now additional dollars are provided by presidential staff personnel (paid by taxpayers) and even the prestige of the presidency is used to gain passage for something that will bring great harm to the families and morals of America. To fight this and other humanist programs, we need to provide after-tax-dollar donations. Give whatever you can afford. After all, if the humanists win, your money will be worthless. You might as well use it now, while there is hope to turn back the ill effects of their programs.

Assist Other Pro-Moral Organizations

When you hear of other groups that share your convictions, lend your moral support. Unfortunately, many Christians refuse to help good causes, unless they or their group are running them. We don't need *prima donnas,* who rush off on their own tangents. Remember, we are in a war that the enemy has been planning for over seventy years. Only dedication, hard work, sacrifice, and cooperation with other moral activists will insure victory. After our triumph over humanism and its dreadful effects on our culture and children, there will be ample time to voice our theological and other differences. But for the next few years, we are obliged to fight a common enemy, and it will take the combined efforts of every morally concerned and informed American.

> The hottest places in Hell are reserved for those who, in times of moral crises, maintain their neutrality.
>
> Dante
> *The Inferno*

Millions of Americans are waking up to the fact that we are facing a moral crises!

Appendix A

Preliminary Questions for Candidates to Determine Their Position on Morals

	YES	NO
1. Do you agree that this country was founded on a belief in God and the moral principles of the Bible? Do you concur that it has been departing from those principles and needs to return to them?	____	____
2. Do you approve of abortion-on-demand when the life of the mother is not in danger?	____	____
3. Do you favor passage of the Equal Rights Amendment?	____	____
4. Do you favor voluntary prayer in the public schools?	____	____
5. Would you favor stricter laws relating to the sale of pornography?	____	____
6. Do you favor stronger laws against the use and sale of hard drugs?	____	____
7. Are you in favor of legalizing marijuana?	____	____
8. Would you favor legalizing prostitution?	____	____
9. Do you favor laws that would increase homosexual rights?	____	____
10. Would you vote to permit known homosexuals to teach school?	____	____
11. Do you favor the right of parents to send their		

children to private schools? _____ _____

12. Do you favor busing schoolchildren out of their
neighborhood to achieve racial integration? _____ _____

13. Do you favor more federal involvement in
education? _____ _____

14. Do you favor capital punishment for capital
offenses? _____ _____

15. Do you favor removal of the tax-exempt status of
churches? _____ _____

16. Do you favor removal of the tax-exempt status of
church-related schools? _____ _____

17. Do you believe that government should remove
children from their parents' homes, except in
cases of physical abuse? _____ _____

18. Do you favor sex education, contraceptives, or
abortions for minors *without* parental consent? _____ _____

19. Except in wartime or dire emergency, would you
vote for government spending that exceeds
revenues? _____ _____

20. Do you favor a reduction in taxes to allow
families more spendable income? _____ _____

21. Do you favor a reduction in government? _____ _____

Appendix B

Recommended Reading List

How Shall We Then Live?
   Francis A. Schaeffer
   Fleming H. Revell Co.
Whatever Happened to the Human Race?
   Francis A. Schaeffer, C. Everett Koop, MD
   Fleming H. Revell
Texas Tech Law Review
   Volume X, Winter 1978, Number 1
   School of Law, Texas Tech University
The SIECUS Circle: A Humanist Revolution
   Claire Chambers
   Western Islands
Change Agents in the Schools
   Barbara M. Morris
   Barbara M. Morris Report
The Assault on the Family
   James M. Parsons, MD
   PRO Media Foundation
Humanism: The Most Dangerous Religion in America
   Homer Duncan
   Christian Focus on Government
A Christian View of Radical Sex Education
   Tim LaHaye
   Family Life Seminars
The Separation Illusion: A Lawyer Examines the First Amendment
   John W. Whitehead
   Mott Media

Education for the Real World
      Henry M. Morris
      Creation Life Publishers
Philosophy and the Christian Faith
      Colin Brown
      Inter-Varsity Press
The Troubled Waters of Evolution
      Henry M. Morris
      Creation Life Publishers
The Philosophy of Humanism
      Corliss Lamont
      Frederick Ungar Publishing Co.
Humanist Manifesto I and II
      Paul Kurtz, editor
      Prometheus Books

Source Notes

1. Dr. Duane Gish, Associate Director, Institute for Creation Research.
2. Ibid.
3. Francis A. Schaeffer, *How Should We Then Live?* (Old Tappan, N.J.: Fleming H. Revell Co., 1976), pp. 51, 52.
4. Ibid.
5. Ibid. p. 55.
6. Will Durant, *The Story of Philosophy,* 2nd ed. (New York: Pocket Books, 1961), p. 203.
7. Schaeffer, p. 121.
8. Ibid. pp. 122–124.
9. John W. Whitehead, *The Separation Illusion* (Milford, MI: Mott Media, 1977), p. 17.
10. Schaeffer, p. 105.
11. Harold O. J. Brown, *The Reconstruction of the Republic* (New Rochelle, N.Y.: Arlington House, 1977), p. 19.
12. Ibid.
13. Ibid. p. 20.
14. Paul A. Kienel, *The Philosophy of Christian School Education* (Whittier, CA: Western Association of Christian Schools), p. 169.
15. Association for Supervision and Curriculum Development, *A New Look at Progressive Education* (Washington: ASCD, 1972), p. 2.
16. Gordon H. Clark, *Dewey* (Philadelphia: The Presbyterian and Reformed Publishing Co., 1960), p. 15.
17. Corliss Lamont, *The Philosophy of Humanism* (New York: Frederick Ungar Publishing Co., 1977), pp. 12, 13.
18. Ibid. p. 116.
19. Ibid. p. 30.

20. Ibid. p. 45.
21. Homer Duncan, *Secular Humanism* (Lubbock, TX: Christian Focus on Government, 1979), p. 16.
22. Ibid. p. 17.
23. Ibid. p. 16.
24. Lamont, p. 83.
25. Ibid. p. 249.
26. Ibid. p. 110.
27. Henry M. Morris, *Education for the Real World* (San Diego: Creation Life Publishers, 1977), p. 82.
28. John W. Whitehead and John Conlan, "The Establishment of the Religion of Secular Humanism and its First Amendment Implications," *Texas Tech Law Review,* X (Winter 1978), p. 54.
29. S. S. Chawla, "A Philosophical Journey to the West," *The Humanist* (September–October 1964), p. 151.
30. James M. Parsons, *The Assault on the Family* (Melbourne, FLA: Pro/Media, 1978), p. 10.
31. Lamont, p. 230.
32. Ibid. p. 232.
33. Ibid. p. 235.
34. Ibid. p. 229.
35. Ibid. p. 241.
36. Ibid. p. 14.
37. Ibid. p. 227.
38. Ibid. p. 14.
39. Schaeffer, p. 224.
40. Lamont, p. 281.
41. Ibid. pp. 42, 43.
42. Claire Chambers, *The SIECUS Circle* (Belmont, HA: Western Islands, 1977), p. 87.
43. Lamont, p. 281.
44. Chambers, pp. 69, 70.
45. Lamont, pp. 281, 282.
46. Ibid. pp. 282, 283.
47. Ibid. pp. 257, 258.
48. Ibid. p. 50.
49. Ibid. pp. 73, 74.
50. Ibid. p. 244.
51. Ibid. p. 82.
52. Ibid. p. 14.

53. Ibid. p. 275.
54. Ibid. p. 283.
55. Humanist Society of San Francisco, *Humanism: What Is It?* (San Francisco: Humanist Society of San Francisco, 1949), p. 3.
56. Lamont, p. 110.
57. *Humanist Manifestos I and II* (Buffalo, N.Y.: Prometheus Books, 1977), p. 3.
58. Ibid. p. 13.
59. Ibid. p. 8.
60. Ibid. p. 16.
61. Ibid.
62. Ibid. p. 8.
63. Ibid.
64. Ibid.
65. Ibid. p. 17.
66. Ibid.
67. Ibid. pp. 18, 19.
68. Ibid. p. 17.
69. Ibid.
70. Ibid. p. 19.
71. Ibid. p. 18.
72. Ibid. p. 9.
73. Ibid. p. 21.
74. Ibid. p. 22.
75. Ibid. p. 20.
76. Ibid. p. 21.
77. Ibid. p. 7.
78. Ibid. pp. 15, 16.
79. Ibid. p. 13.
80. Ibid. pp. 16, 17.
81. Ibid. p. 8.
82. Ibid. p. 14.
83. Ibid. pp. 9, 10.
84. Schaeffer, pp. 132, 133.
85. Ibid. p. 134.
86. Ibid. pp. 134, 135.
87. Dr. Donald B. DeYoung, "Creation Scientists, Part I" (radio transcript no. 345), Institute for Creation Research (September 1978). Copies may be obtained by writing the institute: 2100 Greenfield Dr., El Cajon, CA 92021.

88. *Encyclopedia Britannica* (1975), III, p. 97.
89. Ibid. p. 96.
90. Ibid. p. 97.
91. Schaeffer, p. 135.
92. Ibid. p. 136.
93. DeYoung, no. 346.
94. Ibid.
95. Richard Bliss, "It Takes a Miracle for Evolution," *Christian Heritage Courier* I (March 1979), p. 4. Copies available from: Christian Heritage College, 2100 Greenfield Dr., El Cajon, CA 92021.
96. *See* Francis A. Schaeffer and C. Everett Koop, *Whatever Happened to the Human Race?* (Old Tappan, N.J.: Fleming H. Revell Co., 1979), pp. 102–110.
97. "High School Pupils Find Life Empty, Joyless, Study Says," *San Diego Union,* December 30, 1979.
98. *Education Update* (Heritage Foundation), vol. 3, no. 3, Summer 1979.
99. Ibid.
100. Ibid.
101. Ibid.
102. "The Christian View of Politics," (reprinted essay), pp. 5, 6.
103. Lamont, p. 78.
104. Chambers, p. 92.
105. Ibid.
106. Ibid. pp. 60, 61
107. Ibid. p. 92.
108. Barbara M. Morris, *Change Agents in the Schools* (Ellicott City, MD: The Barbara M. Morris Report, 1979), p. 19.
109. *Humanist Manifestos I and II,* p. 3.
110. Lamont, p. 24.
111. Whitehead and Conlan, p. 19.
112. Ibid. pp. 14, 15.
113. Ibid. pp. 30, 31.
114. Lamont, p. 283.
115. Ibid. p. 6.
116. *Humanist Manifestos I and II,* p. 3.
117. Chambers, p. 82.
118. Lamont, p. 53.
119. Parsons, op. cit.
120. *Texas Tech Law Review,* p. 33.

121. Lamont, p. 274.
122. Ibid. p. 275.
123. Ibid. pp. 282, 283.
124. Schaeffer, p. 225.
125. *San Diego Union,* December 28, 1979.
126. Chambers, p. 62.
127. Ibid. p. 27.
128. Ibid. p. 28.
129. Ibid. p. 28.
130. Ibid. p. 65.
131. Ibid. pp. 66, 67.
132. Ibid. pp. 84, 85.
133. Ibid. p. 85.
134. Ibid.
135. "The Christianity Today-Gallup Poll: An Overview," *Christianity Today,* XXIII (December 21, 1979), p. 14.
136. "We Poll the Pollster," *Christianity Today,* XXIII (December 21, 1979), p. 13.
137. Ibid. p. 12.
138. "Who and Where Are the Evangelicals?" *Christianity Today,* XXIII (December 21, 1979), p. 19.
139. Robert Flood, *America, God Shed His Grace on Thee* (Chicago: Moody Press, 1975), pp. 160, 161.

LaHaye
Temperament
Analysis

- a test to identify your primary and secondary temperaments
- a description of your predominant characteristics
- information regarding your vocational aptitudes and possible vocations suited to you
- recommendations on improving your work habits
- a list of your spiritual gifts, in the order of their priority
- suggestions for where you can best serve in your church
- steps for overcoming your ten greatest weaknesses
- counsel on martial adjustment and parental leadership
- special advice to singles, divorcees, pastors, and the widowed

Your personal 13 to 16 page evaluation letter from Dr. Tim LaHaye will be permanently bound in a handsome vinyl leather portfolio.

... your opportunity
to know yourself
better!